The
Criticism
of
Poetry

The criticism of poetry

S. H. BURTON

Longman

Longman
1724-1974

LONGMAN GROUP LIMITED
London

*Associated companies, branches and representatives
throughout the world*

First published 1950
Twelfth impression 1975

Second Edition 1974
ISBN 0 582 34114 0

Printed in Great Britain
by Lowe & Brydone (Printers) Ltd, Thetford, Norfolk

Contents

Acknowledgments

We are grateful to the following for permission to reproduce copyright material:
The Author's Representatives and Messrs Sidgwick & Jackson Ltd, for a passage from 'The Old Vicarage, Grantchester' from the *Collected Poems of Rupert Brooke*; Mr John Murray for 'Song' from *Selected Poems of R. W. Dixon*; the Author and Messrs Faber & Faber Ltd, for extracts from 'The Metaphysical Poets' from *Selected Essays*, and for 'The Fire Sermon' and 'Preludes' from *Collected Poems* by T. S. Eliot; the Author's Executrix and Messrs Martin Secker & Warburg Ltd, for a passage from 'The Golden Journey to Samarkand' from the *Collected Poems of J. E. Flecker*; Mr Robert Graves for 'The Leveller'; the Trustees of the Hardy Estate and Messrs Macmillan & Co., Ltd, for 'The Darkling Thrush' and 'In the Small Hours' from *The Collected Poems of Thomas Hardy*; the Poet's family and the Oxford University Press for 'Inversnaid', 'Pied Beauty', 'As Kingfishers Catch Fire', 'The Windhover' and passages from 'Felix Randal', 'Spring' and 'The Wreck of the Deutschland' from the *Poems of Gerard Manley Hopkins*; the Oxford University Press for a passage from the introduction to *The Poems of Coleridge*, by Sir Arthur Quiller-Couch in the World's Classics Series; the Society of Authors as the Literary Representatives of the Trustees of the late A. E. Housman; Mrs Bambridge and Messrs Methuen & Co., Ltd, for an extract from 'Danny Deever' from *Barrack Room Ballads* by Rudyard Kipling; Messrs Macmillan & Co., Ltd, for a passage from 'General William Booth enters into Heaven' from *Collected Poems of Vachel Lindsay*; Mr Walter de la Mare and Messrs Faber & Faber Ltd, for 'Silver'; Mrs Wilfred Owen and Messrs Chatto & Windus, for 'Anthem for Doomed Youth' by Wilfred Owen; the Author and Messrs Faber & Faber Ltd, for 'The Express' from *Poems* by Stephen Spender; Faber and Faber Ltd., and Harper & Row, Publishers for the poem 'The Hawk in the Rain' by Ted Hughes from *The Hawk in the Rain*. Copyright © 1957 by Ted Hughes. Reprinted by permission of Faber and Faber Ltd and Harper & Row, Publishers, Inc; J. M. Dent & Sons Ltd., and the Trustees for the copyrights of the late Dylan Thomas for the poem 'A Refusal to Mourn the Death, by Fire, of a Child in London,' by Dylan Thomas from *Collected Poems*; John Murray (Publishers) Ltd., for the poem 'A Child Ill' by John Betjeman from *Collected Poems* by Sir John Betjeman; The Literary Trustees of Walter de la Mare, and the Society of Authors as their representative for the poem 'Hi' from *Collected Poems* by Walter de la Mare; Authors agents for the poem 'I saw a Jolly Hunter' from *Figgie Hobbin* by Charles Causley; Rupert Hart-Davis for the poem 'Pisces' from *Song at the Year's Turning* by R. S. Thomas; the author and Longman Group Ltd for 'Grave by a Holm-Oak' by Stevie Smith from *Scorpion and Other Poems*; Faber & Faber Ltd., for 'Song' from *Collected Poems 1921-1958* by Edwin Muir; Faber & Faber Ltd., and Random House Inc. for Short Ode to the Cuckoo' by W. H. Auden from *Epistle to a Godson and Other Poems*. Copyright © 1972 by W. H. Auden. Reprinted by permission of Faber & Faber Ltd., and Random House Inc; The Executors of the Estate of Harold Owen and Chatto & Windus for the poem 'Arms and the Boy' from *Collected Poems of Wilfred Owen*; Faber & Faber Ltd., for an extract from 'Little Gidding' in *Collected Poems 1909-1962* by T. S. Eliot; Laurence Pollinger Ltd., and the Estate of the Late Mrs Frieda Lawrence for the poem 'Humming-Bird' from *The Complete Poems of D. H. Lawrence* published by William Heinemann Ltd.

We have been unable to trace the copyright holder of the poem 'What the Chairman told Tom' from *Collected Poems* by Basil Bunting and would appreciate receiving any information that would enable us to do so.

Introduction to the second edition

The opportunity to prepare a second edition enables me to make revisions to a book that has stood the test of time pretty well, judging by the numerous impressions through which the first edition has passed. Nevertheless, some alterations are desirable and – the most important change of all – many poems written since 1950 are now included.

Students of literature need help in the writing of criticism. Inability to express critical reactions adequately is frustrating, and intelligent people do not long remain contented to say of a poem, 'I like it because I like it.' Knowledge of critical method is an aid to imaginative reading. Appreciation is enlarged by an understanding of how to apply critical techniques, because the ability to express literary judgements enables enjoyment to be communicated, shared and augmented.

The plan of this book gives theory its due place but lays stress on practical work. The approach to criticism is made through a step-by-step survey of the emotional reactions and thought processes involved in appreciation. Methods of criticism are taught through a close examination of poetic forms and an investigation of the stages through which a critique evolves. Meaning and style are discussed in detail under various headings: intention; tone; versification; diction; imagery. Each chapter contains ample material for practice, concentrating in turn on successive stages of the critical process, the various threads then being interwoven in the full criticism deployed in Chapter 7. Chapter 9 consists entirely of passages for practical criticism, while the appendix on technical terms provides the student with additional tools and increases his critical vocabulary.

A book that has been so long in demand may be supposed to have achieved, in part at least, the aims that its author originally set himself. Foremost among these was the intention to provide readers of poetry with a clear and methodical approach to criticism. No attempt was made to lay down 'rules'; nor did the writer imagine that he could do more than construct a firm base from which critical explorations could be launched. Evidence that students of poetry have been helped in this way has not been lacking. Consequently, in preparing this new edition, I have left the basic plan unchanged while trying to eliminate obscurity and to strengthen the line of argument. The inclusion of more recent poetry gives me great pleasure—for which I thank those poets and publishers (not least my own publishers) who have allowed me to improve the book in this way.

S. H. BURTON

A critical plan

When judging a poem, a critic works to a plan. The aim of this book is to enable you to see that plan and its purpose clearly, and to learn to work to it. Once you have mastered this basic approach you can adapt it to your own ideas and requirements.

We begin here with a summary of the critical plan, and then in successive chapters we investigate each stage of the critical process. Our investigation culminates in the complete criticism of a poem which you will find in Chapter 7.

[A] The critic begins with a general statement of the theme and the tone of the poem as a whole. See Chapters 1 and 2.

[B] Then follows a detailed account of the meaning of the poem, and of the development of the poet's thoughts from the beginning to the end. See Chapter 2.

[C] This section is concerned with the *kind* of theme and the poet's purpose in writing about it. See Chapter 2.

[D] This section deals with the style of the poem. See Chapters 3, 4 and 5.

[E] Here is expressed a final judgement of the poem based on the evidence collected in earlier stages of the critical process. This final judgement should leave the reader with a clear picture of the critic's reactions to the poem as a whole. See Chapter 6.

I
Prejudice, impressions, and judgement

As one reads a poem for the first time, impressions and reactions are constantly forming in the mind. A word stands out from its context by reason of the associations – pleasant or otherwise, and of differing degrees of intensity – which it has for the individual reader; the tongue halts at a phrase, or stumbles over a line; a colour adjective appeals or repels according to the reader's own taste; and so on. By the time the first reading is complete, these transitory, and often half-conscious thoughts and emotions have coalesced to form a first impression of the poem as a whole. The hasty and un-critical reader then plunges into his judgement: 'I like this!' exclaims one. 'This is poor stuff,' says another. For, as Dr I. A. Richards demonstrated so strikingly in his book, *Practical Criticism*, first impressions differ widely and are notoriously unreliable. The word with the unpleasant associations for reader A may have pleasant ones for reader B; C's tongue may glide smoothly over the line that D could not manage; and a colour that E enjoys may not be attractive to F. Here, of course, the hasty reader will break in with, 'Then there's nothing to be done about it, is there? They will never agree about the poem; one likes it, another doesn't; it's all a matter of taste.' That is precisely what it is, a matter of *good* taste; and it should be possible for A and B and the rest of them to find a common standard on which they can base their judgement.

To begin with, they are all falling into the prevalent mistake of forming their opinion on details, considered separately, and not on the poem as a whole. Detail is of enormous importance to the critic, as subsequent chapters of this book will show, but it must always be subordinated to the whole. No one detail can make or mar a poem which is the sum of the details that compose it.

Secondly, they are all judging too hastily. They have not even begun to understand the poem as a whole, but are expressing hasty and purely personal reactions to the one outstanding detail, or details, that they have been struck by in a first reading. A judgement that rests itself on an instinctive or emotional response to a detail is a prejudice and not a true judgement at all. Sound judgement can never precede full understanding;* so the next step to take after the first reading of a poem, is to read the poem again, and again.

While these first readings are taking place, the mind should as far as possible be kept open; not, be it noted, empty, but open to the influence of the poet. The critic should be on the poet's side, not against him, and should thus be sure that any adverse comments that he has to make are made after he has done his best to enter sympathetically and completely into what the poet has said.

We shall have to return to this question of sympathetic reading, but let us now consider an example of the necessity of suspending judgement during the first readings of a poem.

Here is a poem which contains one remarkable defect. Remarkable, that is, in view of the high order of poetry that distinguishes the rest of it. We find it hard to understand how the poet who was capable of achieving the simple beauty of the first two verses, and of conveying so movingly the deep emotion that inspired him, could have been blind to the bathos and banality of the last few words.

> She dwelt among the untrodden ways
> Beside the springs of Dove,

---

*A statement that is complementary to T. S. Eliot's contention that *appreciation* can precede full understanding.

A Maid whom there was none to praise
  And very few to love:

A violet by a mossy stone
  Half hidden from the eye!
—Fair as a star, when only one
  Is shining in the sky.

She lived unknown, and few could know
  When Lucy ceased to be;
But she is in her grave, and, oh,
  The difference to me!

Now, a good criticism of that poem, while yet appreciating its loveliness as a whole, will not shirk mention of the defect, for the fault is serious and indicates a lapse of sensibility on the poet's part. The vigilance that we look for in a great artist has been relaxed, and the acute sensitiveness of a poet to an imagined or real experience and to the words that express this has deserted him. Those five words at the end of the poem constitute more than a detail; they betray a lack of self-criticism, and a temporary failing of the imagination. (It is only fair to add that some critics accept those five words as a bare and strong climax. The reader must decide the point for himself.)

The hasty reader will commit one of two faults when criticising this poem. Either he will allow his enjoyment of the earlier part to blind him to the bathetic ending; or, worse fault still, since it shows the spirit of a caviller, he will concentrate his whole attention on the blunder, and ignore the very real beauty that the poem contains.

Thorough and repeated reading–accompanied of course by sympathy and imagination–will prevent such mistakes in criticism.

There are two main aspects of the critic's function: first, to make clear to his reader the matter of a poem, and the poet's attitude to it; second, to give the reader clearly and unequivocally, the opinion that he (the critic) has formed of the value of that theme, and of the poet's treatment of it. After three careful readings, he should be in a position to begin the first part of his task. At the outset of the criticism of Hardy's poem that is given in Chapter 7, stands a general statement of the theme of the poem, and of the poet's attitude to it. This is, both from the reader's and the critic's point of view, a sound beginning. The reader is informed at once of the interpretation that the critic holds of the matter of the poem. The critic is equally helped, since he has erected a sign-post to guide him in his task. This prefatory general statement is analogous to the title that the précis-writer should invent to epitomise the contents of the passage with which he is dealing. It is, as it were, a yardstick by which he can measure, at every stage, the opinions that he is forming, and the statements that he is making. The first general statement that the critic decides upon may have to be modified in respect of matter when he carries out the careful and detailed verse-by-verse examination of the theme that must precede further judgement. (See Chapter 2.) It may have to be modified in respect of tone when he examines the kind of theme that the poem deals with, and the poet's purpose in writing about it. (See also Chapter 2.) But, whether modified later or not, a generalisation such as this is an invaluable first step in the writing of an appreciation; it is an attempt to catch from the outset the content and spirit of the poem, and acts as a guide to the investigations that must follow it before a final judgement can be passed.

It must be stressed again, however, that this general statement is not to be made until three or more careful readings have given the critic a good general understanding of the poem, and he is thus assured that he is expressing a considered and wisely tentative opinion, and not a half-impression born of prejudice and haste.

So, patiently and carefully, the true critic works; informed always by a desire for truth; animated by a love of poetry; guided by imagination and common sense; and working with purpose and method.

> . . . On a huge hill
> Cragged and steep, Truth stands, and he that will
> Reach her, about must and about must go.

PRACTICAL WORK

1

Read the following passages aloud, and then write down any words or phrases to which you react strongly; describe your reactions (*eg* What does the verse make you think of? Does it suggest something pleasant or grim? What words affect you by their sound, by the images they suggest, by their associations? *etc*) and give where you can, brief reasons for the effect the words have on you. Do not consider your answers at length but give spontaneous replies. It does not matter whether you are 'right' or 'wrong'; the purpose of this practical work is to make you conscious of the immediate and strong reactions that are aroused – sometimes at the half-conscious level – by words, phrases, and sounds.

[A]
> Ruin seize thee, ruthless King!
> Confusion on thy banners wait!
> Tho' fanned by Conquest's crimson wing,
> They mock the air with idle state.
> Helm nor hauberk's twisted mail,
> Nor e'en thy virtues, tyrant, shall avail
> To save thy secret soul from nightly fears,
> From Cambria's curse, from Cambria's tears.

[B]
> A damsel with a dulcimer
> In vision once I saw
> It was an Abyssinian maid,
> And on her dulcimer she played
> Singing of Mount Abora.
> Could I revive within me
> Her symphony and song,
> To such a deep delight 'twould win me,

That with music loud and long,
I would build that dome in air,
That sunny dome! those caves of ice!
And all who heard should see them there,
And all should cry, Beware! Beware!
His flashing eyes, his floating hair!
Weave a circle round him thrice,
And close your eyes with holy dread,
For he on honey-dew hath fed,
And drunk the milk of Paradise.

[C]

Call for the robin-redbreast and the wren,
Since o'er shady groves they hover
And with leaves and flowers do cover
The friendless bodies of unburied men.
Call unto his funeral dole
The ant, the field-mouse, and the mole,
To rear him hillocks that shall keep him warm
And (when gay tombs are robb'd) sustain no harm;
But keep the wolf far hence, that's foe to men,
For with his nails he'll dig them up again.

[D]

Thank Heaven! the crisis—
The danger is past
And the lingering illness
Is over at last—
And the fever called 'Living'
Is conquer'd at last.

Sadly, I know
I am shorn of my strength,
And no muscle I move
As I lie at full length:
But no matter—I feel
I am better at length.

And I rest so composedly
Now, in my bed,
That any beholder

> Might fancy me dead –
> Might start at beholding me,
> Thinking me dead.

[E]

> See how the flowers, as at parade,
> Under their colours stand displayed:
> Each regiment in order grows,
> That of the tulip, pink, and rose.
> But when the vigilant patrol
> Of stars walks round about the pole,
> Their leaves, that to the stalks are curled,
> Seem to their staves the ensigns furled.
> Then in some flower's belovèd hut
> Each bee, as sentinel, is shut,
> And sleeps so too; but if once stirred,
> She runs you through, nor asks the word.

[F]

> What beck'ning ghost, along the moonlight shade
> Invites my steps, and points to yonder glade?
> 'Tis she! – but why that bleeding bosom gored,
> Why dimly gleams the visionary sword?
> O, ever beauteous, ever friendly! tell,
> Is it in Heav'n, a crime to love too well?
> To bear too tender or too firm a heart,
> To act a lover's, or a Roman's part?
> Is there no bright reversion in the sky
> For those who greatly think, or bravely die?

[G]

> When in the chronicle of wasted time
> I see descriptions of the fairest wights,
> And beauty making beautiful old rhyme
> In praise of ladies dead and lovely knights,
> Then, in the blazon of sweet beauty's best,
> Of hand, of foot, of lip, of eye, of brow,
> I see their antique pen would have expressed
> Even such beauty as you master now.
> So all their praises are but prophecies
> Of this our time, all you prefiguring;

> And, for they looked but with divining eyes,
> They had not skill enough you worth to sing;
>   For we, which now behold these present days,
>   Have eyes to wonder, but lack tongues to praise.

2

Read each of the following passages *once*; write a brief statement of the theme of each, and of the poet's attitude to that
theme and to his reader. Then after two more very careful
readings, re-write your statements. Compare the two versions.

[A]

> So we'll go no more a-roving
>   So late into the night
> Though the heart be still as loving,
>   And the moon be still as bright.
>
> For the sword outwears its sheath,
>   And the soul wears out the breast,
> And the heart must pause to breathe,
>   And love itself have rest.
>
> Though the night was made for loving,
>   And the day returns too soon,
> Yet we'll go no more a-roving
>   By the light of the moon.

[B]

> Creep into thy narrow bed,
> Creep, and let no more be said!
> Vain thy onset! all stands fast;
> Thou thyself must break at last.
>
> Let the long contention cease!
> Geese are swans, and swans are geese.
> Let them have it how they will!
> Thou art tired; best be still!
>
> They out-talked thee, hissed thee, tore thee?
> Better men fared thus before thee;
> Fired their ringing shot and passed,
> Hotly charged—and broke at last.

Charge once more, then, and be dumb!
Let the victors, when they come,
When the forts of folly fall,
Find thy body by the wall.

[C]

     The cock is crowing
       The stream is flowing
       The small birds twitter,
       The lake doth glitter,
    The green field sleeps in the sun;
       The oldest and youngest
       Are at work with the strongest;
       The cattle are grazing,
       Their heads never raising;
    There are forty feeding like one!
       Like an army defeated
       The snow hath retreated,
       And now doth fare ill
       On the top of the bare hill;
    The ploughboy is whooping—anon-anon;
       There's joy in the mountains
       There's life in the fountains;
       Small clouds are sailing
       Blue sky prevailing;
    The rain is over and gone!

[D]

Jenny kiss'd me when we met,
   Jumping from the chair she sat in;
Time, you thief, who love to get
   Sweets into your list, put that in!
Say I'm weary, say I'm sad,
   Say that health and wealth have miss'd me,
Say I'm growing old, but add,
   Jenny kiss'd me.

[E]

    Was it a form, a gait, a grace,
      Was it their sweetness merely?

Was it the heaven of a bright face,
    That made me love so dearly?

Was it a skin of milk and snow,
    That soul and senses wounded?
Was't any of these, or all of these,
    Whereon my faith was founded?

Ah, no! 'twas a far deeper part
    Than all the rest that won me:
'Twas a fair-clothed but feigning heart
    I loved, and has undone me.

[F]

Sure thou didst flourish once; and many springs,
    Many bright mornings, much dew, many showers,
Passed o'er thy head; many light hearts and wings,
    Which now are dead, lodged in thy living bowers.

And still a new succession sings and flies;
    Fresh groves grow up, and their green branches shoot
Toward the old and still enduring skies,
    While the low violet thrives at their root.

[G]

Captain, or Colonel, or Knight in Arms,
Whose chance on these defenceless doors may seize,
If deed of honour did thee ever please,
Guard them, and him within protect from harms.
He can requite thee: for he knows the charms
That call fame on such gentle acts as these
And he can spread thy name o'er lands and seas,
Whatever clime the Sun's bright circle warms.
Lift not thy spear against the Muses' bower:
The great Emathian conqueror bid spare
The house of Pindarus, when temple and tower
Went to the ground; and the repeated air
Of sad Electra's poet had the power
To save the Athenian walls from ruin bare.

2
Meaning and intention

After writing his general statement of the theme of the poem, and the poet's attitude to it, the critic is ready to undertake the careful line-by-line examination of the development of the theme that is found in section B of the criticism in Chapter 7. This is a vital stage in appreciation, for it gives the reader that close and intimate contact with the poet's mind and thought without which further advance is impossible.

Bearing in mind his own first statement, he tests it against each verse, and as he follows the development of the poet's thought, he reconsiders his own judgement both of the whole and of each part; taking care as he does so that no one detail is given undue prominence, and, on the other hand, that a vital link in the thought is not ignored in his own epitomising statement.

It is here that the critic must guard himself most carefully against prejudice, haste, and lack of balance. He must preserve a strict sense of proportion, seizing unhesitatingly on what is fundamental, and treating a mere detail with just as much, and just as little emphasis, as a mere detail deserves. Let us take an example of this process.

> Near Martinpuisch that night of hell
> Two men were struck by the same shell,
> Together tumbling in one heap
> Senseless and limp like slaughtered sheep.
>
> One was a pale eighteen-year-old,
> Blue-eyed and thin and not too bold,

Pressed for the war ten years too soon,
The shame and pity of his platoon.

The other came from far-off lands
With bristling chin and whiskered hands,
He had known death and hell before
In Mexico and Ecuador.

Yet in his death this cut-throat wild
Groaned 'Mother! Mother!' like a child,
While that poor innocent in man's clothes
Died cursing God with brutal oaths.

Old Sergeant Smith, kindest of men,
Wrote out two copies there and then
Of his accustomed funeral speech
To cheer the womenfolk of each:–

'He died a hero's death: and we
His comrades of "A" Company
Deeply regret his death; we shall
All deeply miss so true a pal.'

ROBERT GRAVES   *The Leveller*

This poem was set as practical work to a class which was asked to write a general statement of the theme. Many of the students made the same mistake in dealing with the question, their statements reading like this:

This poem describes the death in action of two soldiers; one a mere boy, innocent, inexperienced and afraid; the other a hardened veteran, fearless and rough. The poet ironically tells how, in death, their positions were reversed; the veteran calling piteously for his mother, the boy blaspheming.

That, as far as it goes, is true, but it does not go far enough; and when the students checked their original statement by a thorough examination of each line of the poem, they realised that they had been over-emphasising verse four, and overlooking the significance of verse six. A true statement of the theme must reckon with the *double* irony of the events. You will appreciate this clearly by working through the poem for yourself, paying particular attention to the verses mentioned above.

Each verse then, and each line of a poem must be judged not alone, but in relation to its context, and to the poem as a whole. 'Survey the whole' is a critical maxim, the value of which is too often overlooked.

In Chapter I we referred to the necessity of sympathetic and imaginative reading. However careful the critic's approach to a poem may be, he will never arrive at a true understanding unless he brings these two qualities of sympathy and imagination to his task. The words of a poem are the means whereby a poet seeks to arouse in the reader thoughts and emotions as nearly as possible identical with those that filled the poet's mind as he wrote. They are the symbols of things and ideas, and the reader understands the mind of the poet, only by allowing those symbols to re-create in *his* mind the appropriate things and ideas. There is a double responsibility here: the poet must choose the *right* words; the reader must open his mind to the influence of those words and work *with* the poet. Ruskin put it like this: '. . . be sure you go to the author to get at *his* meaning, not to find yours. Judge it afterwards . . . but ascertain it first.' Especially is this true when one is reading contemporary poetry in which there is frequent use of words and themes which, by reason of their peculiarly intimate associations for the reader, arouse strong and often automatic responses. Here are some lines taken at random from three poems in a selection of modern verse:

> In railway halls, on pavements near the traffic . . .
>
> As from the electric charge of a battery . . .
>
> Its nuts need oil, carbon chokes the valves . . .

Obviously, the critic must be on his guard when judging poems which contain such lines. He must not allow prejudice to interfere with his perception of the meaning of the whole, and he must bring all his powers of imagination and sympathy to the task of discovering *why* the poet wrote about these things, and why no other method of expression would have served his purpose.

Once the meaning of the whole and of the parts has been clearly established and the critic is quite sure that he is working in full imaginative sympathy with the poet, he is in a position to decide the nature of the theme with which the poet is dealing. Criticism can proceed no further until this has been done, for we cannot judge any work of art until we understand clearly what the artist is trying to do, and we must be constant in our endeavour to judge only within our terms of reference. We may as well criticise for his poor batsmanship a man played solely for his bowling, as complain about the lack of humour in *Paradise Lost*. Irrelevance is the surest mark of bad criticism. Having ascertained what the poet is saying, we must then decide what his purpose was in saying it, and judge him solely as he succeeds or fails in that purpose.

According both to its theme and the poet's attitude to that theme, a poem may be classed in one of two groups which may be called 'universal poetry' and 'restricted poetry'. Themes either have a universal application and 'come home to all men's business and their bosoms', or they are restricted in their appeal, satisfying an age, a mood, a group, a temperament; they are fanciful rather than imaginative. Within these broad classifications, there are, of course, degrees, and though we look to universal poetry for the greatest satisfactions that poetry can bring, enduring charm and delight are also to be found in good restricted poetry. In deciding to which of these classes a poem belongs, the subject-matter will, in some cases, be a clear guide; but it is by no means the only guide, nor is it an infallible one, for the poet's attitude to his theme and to his readers, which determines the *tone* of the poem, is as important as the subject-matter. So it is that a poem dealing with love or hate, fear or courage, or any of the other major and eternal human emotions or attitudes to life, may or may not be universal in its appeal, depending entirely on whether the poet has succeeded in achieving that vivid generalisation of ideas and emotions (and expressing this in imperishable language) which ensures an appeal to imaginative readers in any age and under any circumstances. So it is too, that a theme which at first sight seems merely egotistic and personal, may be so enlarged by the poet's vision, fired with his passion, and shaped by his artistry, as to have relevance and meaning for all men. Examples of poems of widely differing subject-matter, some of which are universal, and some of which are restricted, will be useful at this stage.

Pope's 'Rape of the Lock' is at first sight restricted, dealing as it does with conditions obtaining solely in the early eighteenth century. One may well be tempted to wonder what interest a twentieth-century reader can be expected to take in social satire directed against manners and customs long since obsolete. Such a view of the poem, however, is quite inadequate, for Pope in his satirical attack has stripped away flummery and convention, and laid bare the human motives underlying the thoughts and actions of his characters. In so doing, he has provided enduring interest not merely for the student of the period with which he deals, but also for the reader of poetry who loves to find in the magnificence of Pope's heroic couplets a revelation of the permanently human passions, fooleries and poses under the eighteenth-century dress of the protagonists.

That section of Wordsworth's poems of 1807 entitled 'Moods of My Own Mind' provides examples of both universal and restricted poetry. Wordsworth's starting point is very different from Pope's Where the latter is ostensibly impersonal, the former is openly personal, and relies for his appeal on two main factors. First, that the poet, though an exceptional person, is, nevertheless, a representative man, and therefore what interests him interests, too, ordinary men of all ages and in all times. Second, that because he is an exceptional person, the poet feels with a greater intensity than ordinary men and, through his art, is able to give enduring form to the strong emotions that ideas, sights, and incidents, arouse in him. In the poems that follow we see one successful and one unsuccessful example of this process of universalising a personal experience.

[A]

My heart leaps up when I behold
    A Rainbow in the sky:
So was it when my life began;
So is it now I am a Man;
So be it when I shall grow old,
    Or let me die!
The Child is Father of the Man;
And I could wish my days to be
Bound each to each by natural piety.

[B]

Yet are they here?—the same unbroken knot
Of human Beings, in the self-same spot!
    Men, Women, Children, yea the frame
    Of the whole Spectacle the same!
Only their fire seems bolder, yielding light:
Now deep and red, the colouring of night;
    That on their Gipsy-faces falls,
    Their bed of straw and blanket-walls.
—Twelve hours, twelve bounteous hours, are gone while I
Have been a Traveller under open sky,
    Much witnessing of change and chear,
    Yet as I left I find them here!
The weary Sun betook himself to rest.
—Then issued Vesper from the fulgent West,
    Outshining like a visible God
    The glorious path in which he trod.
And now, ascending, after one dark hour,
And one night's diminution of her power,
    Behold the mighty Moon! this way
    She looks as if at them—but they
Regard not her:—oh better wrong and strife,
Better vain deeds or evil than such life!

The silent Heavens have goings on;
The stars have tasks – but these have none.

Poem A is more intensely personal than poem B – and as such might be less interesting were it not so universalised that in speaking for himself, Wordsworth speaks to us all – yet it is a far more valuable experience to read the former than the latter. Nor does this distinction result solely from the subject-matter, for there is intrinsically nothing more 'poetical' in a rainbow than in gipsies. Yet in this first poem Wordsworth has voiced thoughts which are of abiding interest. In the second he has made a few trite observations about the purely suppositious laziness of the gipsies. In Keats's phrase, the rainbow poem is 'a search after truth', whereas the gipsy poem is not. And be it noted that the cardinal artistic weakness of the second poem is not that it is restricted, but that in attempting universality with inadequate material and a complacent attitude, Wordsworth inevitably achieved bathos.

Let us take another example of a satirical poem to contrast with Pope's. *Hudibras*, by Samuel Butler, one of the most sustained flights of invective in the English language, is a poem which no *specialist* student either of English Literature or of English History can afford to ignore. Many of its lines have become proverbial, so universal *at moments* is its appeal.

> Such as do build their faith upon
> The holy text of pike and gun.
>
> Compound for sins they are inclined to
> By damning those they have no mind to.
>
> Quoth she, I've heard old cunning stagers
> Say, Fools for arguments use wagers.
>
> For Justice, though she's painted blind,
> Is to the weaker side inclined.

Despite such enduring epigrams, however, *Hudibras* is an example of good restricted poetry. The subject-matter of the poem and the author's attitude to it are so specialised that it cannot make that *broad* appeal that we expect from universal poetry. The student of the seventeenth century must read it, the scholar must read it; the lover of poetry who does not read it will not thereby impoverish his appreciation of the greatest poetry.

Here is a delightful lyric which Cowper enclosed in a letter to a friend.

> The swallows in their torpid state
>   Compose their useless wing,
> And bees in hives as idly wait
>   The call of early spring.
>
> The keenest frost that binds the stream,
>   The wildest wind that blows,
> Are neither felt nor feared by them,
>   Secure of their repose:
>
> But man, all feeling and awake,
>   The gloomy scene surveys;
> With present ills his heart must ache,
>   And pant for brighter days.
>
> Old Winter, halting in the mead,
>   Bids me and Mary mourn;
> But lovely Spring peeps o'er his head,
>   And whispers your return.
>
> Then April with her sister May
>   Shall chase him from the bowers,
> And weave fresh garlands every day,
>   To crown the smiling hours.
>
> And if a tear that speaks regret
>   Of happier times appear,
> A glimpse of joy that we have met
>   Shall shine, and dry the tear.

This is a charming and simple poem, yet it is too, a restricted one, as it was meant to be. Because the result is so completely in harmony with the poet's intentions, it is an artistic success. There is, however, nothing here to modify our experience permanently and greatly; nothing to sink so deeply into our consciousness that, having read the poem, we look at Spring in a new way ever after, our attitude to that season enriched and deepened by the poem. Compare the effect of Cowper's poem with the effect of these lines from *The Winter's Tale* and you will learn much about the difference between universal and restricted poetry.

> . . . daffodils,
> That come before the swallow dares, and take
> The winds of March with beauty; violets dim
> But sweeter than the lids of Juno's eyes
> Or Cytherea's breath; pale primroses,
> That die unmarried, ere they can behold
> Bright Phoebus in his strength – a malady
> Most incident to maids.

Cowper was expressing delightfully a mood which seized on him as he anticipated the arrival of his friend in the Spring: Shakespeare was giving deathless utterance to Everyman's emotions when confronted with the fleeting and poignant beauty of the young year. See how deliberately he widens the scope of his theme in the last line and a half.

Finally, let us take two examples of poetry which will remove the false idea that because a poem is intended to be universal it is by that very fact superior to one which is intended to be restricted. We distinguish between the two kinds of poetry because it is essential to criticise only with a clear realisation of what the poet is trying to do, not because the restricted poem is necessarily inferior to the universal one. In the final judgement everything depends upon the poet's execution of the task that he has set himself: his preservation of harmony between his means and his ends. A restricted poem may be of a high order of art *in that it is exactly what it was planned to be*. It is when the poet's theme and his treatment of it are in marked disharmony that the poem – whether intended to be universal or restricted – is an artistic failure. The consequences of such disharmony will be treated fully in the chapters on style.

Here, first, is an example of a poem whose theme has potentially a universal significance, and whose writer is alive to that potentiality.

> Mountain gorses, ever golden,
> Cankered not the whole year long!
> Do ye teach us to be strong,
> Howsoever pricked and holden
> Like your thorny blooms, and so
> Trodden on by rain and snow,
> Up the hill-side of this life, as bleak as where ye grow?

> Mountain blossoms, shining blossoms,
> Do ye teach us to be glad
> When no summer can be had,
> Blooming in our inward bosoms?
> Ye, whom God preserveth still,
> Set as lights upon a hill,
> Tokens to the wintry earth that Beauty liveth still!

> Mountain gorses, do ye teach us
> From that academic chair
> Canopied with azure air,
> That the wisest word man reaches
> Is the humblest he can speak?
> Ye, who live on mountain peak,
> Yet live low along the ground, beside the grasses meek!

> Mountain gorses, since Linnaeus
> Knelt beside you on the sod,
> For your beauty thanking God, –
> For your teaching, ye should see us
> Bowing in prostration new!
> Whence arisen, – if one or two
> Drops be on our cheeks – O world, they are not tears
> but dew.

And now we have a poem which is restricted in theme and in treatment, the poet clearly recognising the value of his subject, yet refusing to stretch his material beyond its proper limits.

THE MOWER TO THE GLOW-WORMS

Ye living lamps, by whose dear light
The nightingale does sit so late,
And studying all the summer night,
Her matchless songs does meditate:

Ye country comets, that portend
No war nor prince's funeral,
Shining unto no higher end
Than to presage the grass's fall:

Ye glow-worms, whose officious flame
To wandering mowers shows the way,
That in the night have lost their aim,
And after foolish fires do stray:

Your courteous lights in vain you waste,
Since Juliana here is come,
For she my mind hath so displaced
That I shall never find my home.

Which is the better poem, and why?

We can then at the outset distinguish between universal and restricted poetry, realising that in making that distinction we are concerned at least as much with the poet's attitude to his theme, as with the theme itself.

If we substitute 'poem' for the word 'book' in the following quotations, we shall have a clearer guide still to this all-important distinction. First, Bacon on the subject: 'Some books are to be tasted, others to be swallowed, and some few are to be chewed and digested'; and next Ruskin:

For all books are divisible into two classes, the books of the hour, and the books of all time. Mark this distinction—it is not one of quality only. It is not merely the bad book that does not last, and the good one that does. It is a distinction of species. There are good books of the hour, and bad ones for all time.

Before he can judge the artistic merit of any poem, the critic, it is now clear, must decide whether the theme (and the poet's attitude to it) is universal or restricted, and further and in greater detail, whether being one or the other, it is ironic, satirical, trivial, fantastic, humorous, allegorical, symbolic, descriptive, narrative, lyrical, and so forth. (You will find more about the kinds of poetry in the Appendix.) To discover the nature of the theme and the poet's attitude towards it, he should ask himself questions such as these. What relevance has this poem for me? Is it a pleasant trifle dealing lightly with an idle theme, or is it an attempt to reveal a truth about life as the poet sees it? Is it concerned with the external features of a way of life long since dead, or with human situations and passions which underlay that manner of life? Is it a merely personal outburst, of interest solely in so far as it reveals the personality of the poet – and is that personality worth revealing? – or is it concerned with the emotions and motives that the poet, and I, and every man have in common? Are the emotions expressed valuable and compelling, or are they artificial and in excess of the stimulus? Does this poem touch the whole of my life, or only a part of it? Does it profoundly modify my sensibilities, or appeal strongly to a mood and a moment? Is this poem what its writer meant it to be, or has he aimed too high and missed his mark?

These are but a few of the questions that may be asked when deciding the nature of the theme of a poem and the poet's attitude to that theme; and practice in the art of criticism will suggest a wider range of questions to you. But the important thing to remember is that such questions must be asked and answered before you can proceed with your criticism for, again it must be stressed, *you can only judge a poet in the light of what he is trying to do*.

PRACTICAL WORK

1

Pick out the key stanzas or lines in the following, and show
clearly the relationship of the rest of the poem to these. Bring
out forcibly in your answers the climaxes or contrasts that the
poet is making in each case.

[A]

Toll for the brave –
The brave! that are no more:
   All sunk beneath the wave,
Fast by their native shore.
   Eight hundred of the brave,
Whose courage was well tried,
   Had made the vessel heel
And laid her on her side;
   A land-breeze shook the shrouds,
And she was overset:
   Down went the Royal George,
With all her crew complete.

   Toll for the brave –
Brave Kempenfelt is gone,
   His last sea-fight is fought,
His work of glory done.
   It was not in the battle,
No tempest gave the shock,
   She sprang no fatal leak,
She ran upon no rock;
   His sword was in the sheath,
His fingers held the pen,
   When Kempenfelt went down
With twice four hundred men.

   Weigh the vessel up,
Once dreaded by our foes,
   And mingle with your cup
The tears that England owes;
   Her timbers yet are sound,
And she may float again,

23

Full charg'd with England's thunder,
And plough the distant main;
But Kempenfelt is gone,
His victories are o'er;
And he and his eight hundred
Must plough the wave no more.

[B]

It was roses, roses, all the way,
    With myrtle mixed in my path like mad:
The house-roofs seemed to heave and sway,
    The church-spires flamed, such flags they had,
A year ago on this very day.

The air broke into a mist with bells,
    The old walls rocked with the crowd and cries.
Had I said, 'Good folk, mere noise repels—
    But give me your sun from yonder skies!'
They had answered, 'And afterward, what else?'

Alack, it was I who leaped at the sun
    To give it my loving friends to keep!
Nought man could do, have I left undone:
    And now you see my harvest, what I reap
This very day, now a year is run.

There's nobody on the house-tops now—
    Just a palsied few at the windows set;
For the best of the sight is, all allow,
    At the Shambles' Gate—or, better yet,
By the very scaffold's foot, I trow.

I go in the rain, and, more than needs,
    A rope cuts both my wrists behind;
And I think, by the feel, my forehead bleeds,
    For they fling, whoever has a mind,
Stones at me for. my year's misdeeds.

Thus I entered, and thus I go!
    In triumphs, people have dropped down dead.
'Paid by the World,—what dost thou owe
    Me?'—God might question; now instead,
'Tis God shall repay: I am safer so.

[C]

What's life but full of care and doubt,
  With all its fine humanities,
With parasols we walk about,
  Long pigtails and such vanities.

We plant pomegranate trees and things,
  And go in gardens sporting,
With toys and fans of peacock's wings,
  To painted ladies courting.

We gather flowers of every hue,
  And fish in boats for fishes,
Build summer-houses painted blue,
  But life's as frail as dishes.

Walking about their groves of trees,
  Blue bridges and blue rivers,
How little thought them two Chinese,
  They'd both be smashed to shivers!

[D]

Sweet, be not proud of those two eyes,
Which star-like sparkle in their skies;
Nor be you proud, that you can see
All hearts your captives, yours yet free.
Be you not proud of that rich hair,
Which wantons with the love-sick air;
Whenas that ruby which you wear,
Sunk from the tip of your soft ear,
Will last to be a precious stone
When all your world of beauty's gone.

[E]

When I consider how my light is spent
Ere half my days in this dark world and wide
And that one talent which is death to hide
Lodged with me useless, though my soul more bent
To serve therewith my Maker, and present
My true account, lest he returning chide,
'Doth God exact day-labour, light denied?'

I fondly ask; but Patience, to prevent
That murmur, soon replies, 'God doth not need
Either man's work, or his own gifts. Who best
Bear his mild yoke, they serve him best: His state
Is kingly. Thousands at his bidding speed
And post o'er land and ocean without rest:
They also serve who only stand and wait.'

2

After several thorough readings of the following, decide
whether the poems are universal or restricted. Give full reasons
for your decisions, remembering that the poet's attitude to the
theme is at least as important as the subject-matter itself.

[A]

Feed on, my flocks, securely
Your shepherd watcheth surely:
Run about, my little lambs,
Skip and wanton with your dams,
    Your loving herd with care will tend ye.
Sport on, fair flocks, at pleasure,
Nip Vesta's flow'ring treasure;
I myself will duly hark,
When my watchful dog doth bark;
From wolf and fox I will defend ye.

[B]

A gentle squire would gladly entertain
Into his house some trencher-chaplain;
Some willing man that might instruct his sons,
And that would stand to good conditions.
First, that he lie upon the truckle-bed,
While his young master lieth o'er his head.
Secondly, that he do, on no default,
Ever presume to sit above the salt.
Third, that he never change his trencher twice.
Fourth, that he use all comely courtesies;
Sit bare at meals, and one half rise and wait.
Last, that he never his young master beat,

But he must ask his mother to define
How many jerks she would his breech should line.
All these observed, he would contented be.
To give five marks and winter livery.

[C]

I met a traveller from an antique land
Who said: two vast and trunkless legs of stone
Stand in the Desert. Near them on the sand,
Half sunk, a shattered visage lies, whose frown
And wrinkled lip and sneer of cold command
Tell that its sculptor well those passions read
Which yet survive, stamped on these lifeless things,
The hand that mocked them and the heart that fed;
And on the pedestal these words appear:
'My name is Ozymandias, king of kings:
Look on my works, ye mighty, and despair!'
Nothing beside remains. Round the decay
Of that colossal wreck, boundless and bare
The lone and level sands stretch far away.

[D]

Even such is time, that takes on trust
Our youth, our joys, our all we have,
And pays us but with age and dust;
Who, in the dark and silent grave,
When we have wandered all our ways,
Shuts up the story of our days.
But from this earth, this grave, this dust,
My God shall raise me up, I trust.

[E]

Behold! a giant am I!
    Aloft here in my tower,
    With my granite jaws I devour
The maize, and the wheat, and the rye,
    And grind them into flour.

I look down over the farms;
    In the fields of grain I see
    The harvest that is to be,

And I fling to the air my arms,
    For I know it is all for me.

I hear the sound of flails
    Far off, from the threshing-floors
    In barns, with their open doors,
And the wind, and the wind in my sails,
    Louder and louder roars.

I stand here in my place,
    With my foot on the rock below,
    And whichever way it may blow
I meet it face to face,
    As a brave man meets his foe.

And while we wrestle and strive,
    My master, the miller, stands
    And feeds me with his hands;
For he knows who makes him thrive,
    Who makes him lord of lands.

On Sundays I take my rest;
    Church-going bells begin
    Their low, melodious din;
I cross my arms on my breast,
    And all is peace within.

3

Read these poems and the criticisms given of each. Give your opinion of the criticisms, showing clearly where and why you agree or disagree with them.

[A]

Proud Maisie is in the wood,
    Walking so early;
Sweet Robin sits on the bush,
    Singing so rarely.

'Tell me, thou bonny bird,
When shall I marry me?'
–'When six braw gentlemen
    Kirkward shall carry ye.'

> 'Who makes the bridal bed,
>   Birdie, say truly?'
> –'The gray-headed sexton
>   That delves the grave duly.'
>
> 'The glow-worm o'er grave and stone
>   Shall light thee steady;
> The owl from the steeple sing
>   Welcome, proud lady!'

It is a pity that the poet did not tell a plain tale plainly. He suggests a mystery without making clear what the mystery is, and the poem has the appearance of an annoying fragment rather than a complete story.

[B]

> After the first powerful plain manifesto
> The black statement of pistons, without more fuss
> But gliding like a queen, she leaves the station.
> Without bowing and with restrained unconcern
> She passes the houses which humbly crowd outside,
> The gasworks and at last the heavy page
> Of death, printed by gravestones in the cemetery.
> Beyond the town there lies the open country
> Where, gathering speed, she acquires mystery,
> The luminous self-possession of ships on ocean.
> It is now she begins to sing–at first quite low,
> Then loud, and at last with a jazzy madness–
> The song of her whistle screaming at curves,
> Of deafening tunnels, brakes, innumerable bolts.
> And always light, aerial, underneath
> Goes the elate metre of her wheels.
> Steaming through metal landscape on her lines
> She plunges new eras of wild happiness
> Where speed throws up strange shapes, broad curves
> And parallels clean like the steel of guns.
> At last, further than Edinburgh or Rome,
> Beyond the crest of the world, she reaches night
> Where only a low streamline brightness
> Of phosphorus on the tossing hills is white.

29

>   Ah, like a comet through the flame she moves entranced
>   Wrapt in her music no bird song, no, nor bough
>   Breaking with honey buds, shall ever equal.

We cannot believe that the departure of a railway engine is a fit subject for poetry, and this disbelief is enhanced by our utter inability to see any beauty in pistons, tunnels, brakes, bolts, or any of the other stock-in-trade of the modern poet.

[c]

>   Come live with me and be my love,
>   And we will all the pleasures prove
>   That hills and valleys, dale and field,
>   And all the craggy mountains yield.
>
>   There we will sit upon the rocks
>   And see the shepherds feed their flocks,
>   By shallow rivers, to whose falls
>   Melodious birds sing madrigals.
>
>   There I will make thee beds of roses
>   And a thousand fragrant posies,
>   A cap of flowers, and a kirtle
>   Embroidered all with leaves of myrtle;
>
>   A gown made of the finest wool,
>   Which from our pretty lambs we pull,
>   Fair linèd slippers for the cold,
>   With buckles of the purest gold.
>
>   A belt of straw and ivy buds,
>   With coral clasps and amber studs:
>   And if these pleasures may thee move,
>   Come live with me and be my love.
>
>   The shepherds swains shall dance and sing
>   For thy delight each May-morning:
>   If these delights thy mind may move,
>   Then live with me and be my love.

It is impossible to take this utterly unrealistic poem seriously.

Its artificiality is most unpleasing, especially in view of the potential dignity of its theme.

[D]

> The feathers of the willow
> Are half of them grown yellow
>   Above the swelling stream;
>
> And ragged are the bushes
> And rusty now the rushes,
>   And wild the clouded gleam.
>
> The thistle now is older,
> His stalk begins to moulder,
>   His head is white as snow;
> The branches all are barer,
> The linnet's song is rarer,
>   The robin pipeth now.

No useful lesson can be drawn from this poem. The writer has a descriptive knack, but fails to give any real and lasting significance to what he observes.

[E]

> If, in the month of dark December,
>   Leander, who was nightly wont
> (What maid will not the tale remember?)
>   To cross the stream, broad Hellespont!
>
> If, when the wintry tempest roar'd,
>   He sped to Hero, nothing loth,
> And thus of old thy current pour'd,
>   Fair Venus! how I pity both!
>
> For me, degenerate modern wretch,
>   Though in the genial month of May,
> My dripping limbs I faintly stretch,
>   And think I've done a feat to-day.
>
> But since he cross'd the rapid tide,
>   According to the doubtful story,
> To woo,–and–Lord knows what beside,
>   And swam for Love, as I for Glory;

31

'Twere hard to say who fared the best:
   Sad mortals! thus the gods still plague you!
He lost his labour, I my jest;
   For he was drown'd, and I've the ague.

The story of Hero and Leander is one that has for centuries held man's imagination and sense of romance. The poet, however, has not succeeded in appealing to either of these faculties: his treatment of the theme is not what one expects.

3
Style: Versification*

There need be no undue mystery about style, nor need the beginner in literary criticism approach this aspect of his task with greater hesitancy than when tackling meaning. Though it is true that the full appreciation of good style needs a developed judgement and wide reading – as Longinus put it, 'Judgement of style is the last and ripest fruit of much experience' – yet we can from the very beginning cultivate our taste, and advance towards true appreciation by considering form only in relation to matter and intention.

The only sound way to consider style is to regard it as something functional. In trying to distinguish between good and bad style, remember what was said in Chapter 2 about the supreme importance of harmony between the task that the poet has set himself, and the means by which he seeks to accomplish it: in other words, look constantly for a proper relationship between means and ends. The truest way of judging style is to ask this question. Is the medium of expression that the poet has chosen the best one for realising the goal that he has set himself? Let us express this as simply and as vividly as possible by tabulating the stages through which our enquiry must pass if we are to arrive at a true judgement of a poem.

1 What is the poet saying?

2 What is his intention in saying it?

3 Does his method of saying it help or hinder that intention?

*When reading this and the subsequent chapters on style, you will find it helpful to refer to the Appendix for an explanation of any technical terms that you do not understand.

When we come to our final judgement we shall have to add further questions in order to complete the critical process, but the three listed above take us as far as our judgement of the style. Throughout these chapters on style, whether we are concerned with versification, with diction, or with imagery, you will find this fundamental approach: are the means suitable to the ends?

Even before you begin to read a poem, you are conscious by the very *look* of it that it is of a particular style. For example, this chapter has, up to now, consisted of prose. Here is some poetry:

> The curfew tolls the knell of parting day,
>   The lowing herd winds slowly o'er the lea,
> The ploughman homeward plods his weary way,
>   And leaves the world to darkness and to me.

and some more poetry:

> Out upon it, I have loved
>   Three whole days together;
> And am like to love three more,
>   If it prove fine weather.

and some more:

> At the round earth's imagined corners, blow
> Your trumpets, angels, and arise, arise
> From death, you numberless infinities
> Of souls, and to your scattered bodies go,
> All whom the flood did, and fire shall o'erthrow,
> All whom war, dearth, age, agues, tyrannies,
> Despair, law, chance, hath slain, and you, whose eyes
> Shall behold God, and never taste death's woe.

and more:

> O raging seas
>   and mighty Neptune's reign,
> In monstrous hills
>   that throwest thyself so high,

That with thy floods
   dost beat the shores of Spain,
And break the cliffs
   that dare thy force envy.

Now, you have only to use your eyes to see that there is a difference in style between the prose in which this chapter is written, and the poetry which we have just quoted. Using your eyes again, you will see that there is, too, a great difference in style between the individual poems themselves. The very arrangement of the lines which catches the eye as soon as we look at poetry draws our attention to this question of form.

But there is very much more in reading poetry than merely looking. Poetry is meant to be read aloud, and sound, far more than sight, gives it its form. Test this for yourselves. Here are two lines of exactly equal length, and sight alone would be powerless to detect the enormous difference in form that distinguishes each from the other. Read them aloud and you will at once realise that they are written in two different styles.

[A]

The Lotos blooms below the barren peak.

[B]

Shakespeare was of us, Milton was for us.

Let us now point the contrast by quoting more of the verses from which these lines are taken.

[A]

The Lotos blooms below the barren peak:
The Lotos blows by every winding creek:
All day the wind breathes low with mellower tone:
Thro' every hollow cave and alley lone
Round and round the spicy downs the yellow Lotos-dust
   is blown.

[B]

We that had loved him so, followed him, honoured him,
   Lived in his mild and magnificent eye,

Learned his great language, caught his clear accents,
　Made him our pattern to live and to die!
Shakespeare was of us, Milton was for us,
　Burns, Shelley, were with us,–they watch from their graves!
He alone breaks from the van and the freemen,
　–He alone sinks to the rear and the slaves!

The aspect of style that we are so forcibly confronted with here is rhythm. All poetry is rhythmical, and a blend of stress and quantity forms the basis of English verse rhythms. Rhythm is a fundamental phenomenon of life, and it is poetry's dependence upon it that helps to make poetry so powerful an influence in the lives of men. The ebb and flow of the tides and seasons, the recurrence of waking and sleeping, the rhythm of breathing, the beat of the heart–all these vital processes exhibit the same clearly marked feature of periodicity which also characterises poetry, dancing, marching, and music. There is, of course, a rhythm in prose, but the word sequences of poetry have a regular *pattern* of rhythm; a beat which throbs through the lines, and which varies in intensity and mode of appeal as greatly as the rhythms of music where, for example, the monotonous beat of the tom-tom differs from the highly-wrought artistry of classical syncopation, yet both carry a powerful rhythmic appeal. Rhythmic satisfaction is aroused in poetry, as in music, both by the perception of recurring patterns of rhythm, and by variety within those patterns.

There is considerable controversy about the metrical basis of English poetry and about the symbols and terms that should be employed in scansion. We should perhaps attempt here to clarify some of these issues. It is important first of all to be clear about the relationship between metre and rhythm, for these terms are not synonymous. As George Sampson has said, 'Metre is the skeleton, rhythm the living body'. Metre is the mechanical basis of the line; rhythm is the full and free expression of the poet's thought, based upon, but often transcending, metrical requirements. A great poet uses metre as his servant, preserving a metrical pattern so as to secure a form and discipline for his work, but varying that pattern by super-imposing a rhythmical pattern which is distinctly and uniquely personal. Poems written in the same *metre* may have very different *rhythms*. We shall return to this subject later in this chapter and in the practical work that follows it. Before we can do so, however, we must try to establish a clear agreement about scansion in general.

English scansion is based on stress (or 'accent'). Confusion sometimes arises from the fact that the symbols and terms often used to describe English rhythms and metres are derived from Greek (and Latin) prosody which was based on quantity. Greek verse was written in 'long' and 'short' syllables with a fixed quantitative relationship between the two, the long syllable being equal to two short syllables.

In English scansion, where stress is dominant, the Greek symbols for 'long' and 'short' (— and ‿) can be applied only to stressed and unstressed (or 'slack') syllables. They cannot have quantitative significance in English prosody.

This is made clear by an illustration. The words 'fearsome' and 'pretty' have exactly the same notation in English scansion:

$$\overline{\text{fear}} \ \overset{\cup}{\text{some}}$$

$$\overline{\text{pret}} \ \text{ty}$$

But if the 'classical' signs are used with their *original* (*ie* quantitative) meaning, the scansion is:

$$\overline{\text{fear}} \ \overset{\cup}{\text{some}}$$

$$\overset{\cup}{\text{pret}} \ \overset{\cup}{\text{ty}}$$

Nowadays, there is general agreement that the classical symbols are confusing when used in English scansion, where the terms 'longs' and 'shorts' are inappropriate. Instead of using — to mark a stressed syllable ╱ is preferred; and × replaces ‿ for a slack or unstressed syllable:

fear some
pret ty

Use of those symbols breaks down the false parallel between classical and English prosody. It has the further advantage of providing a symbol for part-stressed syllables. The sign ＼ can be used for a syllable which, while not slack, does not carry a full stress. Any system of English scansion must be as flexible as the verse which it is describing; a feature of English poetry being the frequent modification of the basic metrical patterns by the speech rhythms that override them.

It will be helpful at this point to provide an example scanned according to the system just advocated.

> Yet hope not Life from Grief or Danger free,
> Nor think the Doom of Man revers'd for thee.
> Deign on the passing World to turn thine Eyes
> And pause awhile from Letters to be wise;
> There mark what Ills the Scholar's Life assail,
> Toil, Envy, Want, the Patron and the Jail.
> See Nations slowly wise, and meanly just,
> To buried Merit raise the tardy Bust:
> If Dreams yet flatter; once again attend,
> Hear Lydiat's Life and Galileo's End.

That passage from Samuel Johnson's *The Vanity of Human Wishes* is written in heroic couplets (iambic pentameters, rhyming aa, bb, cc, *etc*). The beat is steady and, on the whole, regular. Yet notice how often—and especially towards the end—the strong emotion demands modification of the regular × ∕ × ∕ × ∕ × ∕ × ∕ metre. Read the lines aloud and hear the speech rhythm overriding the metrical pattern. Sense and feeling break through and re-mould the formal metre. (You may want to vary the offered scansion in places. *Your* reading may differ from that proposed above.)

The two lines of poetry that we quoted earlier provide illustrations of the two main kinds of 'time' in English poetry. [A]

DUPLE TIME

Thĕ Lót|ŏs bloóms | bĕlòw | thĕ bárr|ĕn peák |

[B]

TRIPLE TIME

Shákespĕare wăs | ŏf ŭs, | Míltŏn wăs | fŏr ŭs. |

In A each foot consists of two syllables, one stressed and one slack; in B two of the four feet are trisyllabic. Notice how an increase in the number of *stressed* syllables slows the line down, and how a decrease quickens it. Duple time may be either iambic or trochaic; triple time is either anapaestic or dactylic. Movement from duple to triple time or vice-versa is often found within the lines of a single poem. This gives an effect of extreme flexibility and sensitive modulations of tone which enhances the music and enriches the meaning, especially of a lyric. Take as an example of this these lines from Shelley's *Ode to Night*, which R. C. Trevelyan quotes in his suggestive essay *Classical and English Verse-Structure* (*English Association Essays and Studies, Vol. XVI*).

> Swiftly walk o'er the western wave,
>   Spirit of Night!
> Out of the misty eastern cave,
> Where, all the long and lone daylight,
> Thou wovest dreams of joy and fear,
> That make thee terrible and dear,—
>   Swift be thy flight!
>
> Wrap thy form in a mantle gray,
>   Star-inwrought!
> Blind with thy hair the eyes of Day;
> Kiss her until she be wearied out,

> Then wander o'er city, and sea, and land,
> Touching all with thine opiate wand—
>   Come, long-sought!

Notice here the great pleasure given by the movement from triple to duple time and back again to triple, and the way in which these time changes correspond to emotional movement in the poem. Scan, and describe the effect of, the last line in each stanza.

Though stress (or *accent*) is dominant in English rhythms, quantity plays an important part. Let us return again to our original examples.

[A]

> The Lótos bloóms belòw the bárren péak.

[B]

> Shákespeare was óf us, Mílton was fór us.

Notice that in A the stress falls on long syllables, whereas in B the accent comes on sharp, quick vowel sounds. This reinforces the stress effect by further slowing the movement of A and hastening that of B. Here are extracts from *L'Allegro* and *Il Penseroso* which further illustrate the interplay of stress and quantity.

[A]

> To hear the lark begin his flight,
> And, singing, startle the dull night,
> From his watch-tower in the skies,
> Till the dappled dawn doth rise;
> Then to come in spite of sorrow,
> And at my window bid good-morrow,
> Through the sweet-briar or the vine,
> Or the twisted eglantine.

[B]

> And, missing thee, I walk unseen
> On the dry smooth-shaven green,

> To behold the wandering moon,
> Riding near her highest noon,
> Like one that had been led astray
> Through the heaven's wide pathless way,
> And oft, as if her head she bowed,
> Stooping through a fleecy cloud.
> Oft on a plat of rising ground,
> I hear the far-off curfew sound,
> Over some wide-watered shore,
> Swinging slow with sullen roar.

Both A and B are written in iambic tetrameters but their rhythmic effect is very different. In A the stressed syllables are sharp and quick, in B the accent tends to fall on long and sonorous syllables. Hence A is a perfect medium of expression for the light-hearted man, whereas the sound of B sustains and enriches the theme of 'pleasing melancholy'.

B illustrates, too, the importance of 'counterpointing'. We said earlier that rhythmic satisfaction arises from the ear's perception both of recurring patterns and of variety within those patterns. The basis of B is duple time with a rising rhythm, but very often rhythmic and metrical stress-patterns are counterpointed, thus securing variety within regularity, freedom within form. The double satisfaction of pattern and innovation is achieved by lines such as:

> And óft as íf her héad she bówed,
> Stóoping thróugh a fléecy clóud.
> Óft on a plát of rísing gróund,
> I héar the fár-òff cúrfew sóund,
> Óver sóme wíde-wátered shóre,
> Swínging slów with súllen róar.

In line two the metrical pattern should be

$$\times \diagup \times \diagup \times \diagup \times \diagup$$

but to read it thus would be a blatant misreading, for the

speech accent is counterpointed against it, and the line is in *falling* rhythm though still in duple time. There are three other examples of this in this short passage. The intense rhythmic satisfaction obtained from counterpointing arises from the fact that metrical and rhythmic patterns are juxtaposed in such a way that the stresses suddenly fall just where the ear did *not* expect them. Then the rhythmic pattern is again synchronised with the metrical, and the other satisfaction of a gratified expectation is yielded to the ear.

These verses from Scott's *Bonny Dundee* provide some vivid illustrations of rhythmic effect.

To the Lords of Convention 'twas Claver'se who spoke,
'Ere the King's crown shall fall there are crowns to be broke;
So let each Cavalier who loves honour and me,
Come follow the bonnet of Bonny Dundee.
'Come fill up my cup, come fill up my can,
  Come saddle your horses, and call up your men;
  Come open the West Port, and let me gang free,
  And it's room for the bonnets of Bonny Dundee!'

He waved his proud hand, and the trumpets were blown,
The kettle-drums clash'd, and the horsemen rode on,
Till on Ravelston's cliffs and on Clermiston's lee
Died away the wild war-notes of Bonny Dundee.
'Come fill up my cup, come fill up my can,
  Come saddle the horses and call up the men,
  Come open your gates, and let me gae free,
  For it's up with the bonnets of Bonny Dundee!'

A stirring tale told in rising triple time with the very sound of hoof-beats, kettle-drums, and trumpets echoing through the lines: all the romance of the theme reflected in the rhythm. Yet not so artless perhaps as one might think. The writer, for example, was at a loss to account for the particularly exciting · effect of the last line in each verse, until he realised that in each case it is at least one syllable longer than any of the other lines of the chorus, but has only the same number of stressed

syllables and begins, not with a duple, but a triple-time foot;
thus its tempo is quickened, and it rushes out energetically,
giving force to the defiance it expresses after the more
deliberate utterance of its three immediate predecessors. One
hears the measured canter of the horses breaking into a wild
gallop as the gate is forced and the open country reached.

Take for contrast, Wolfe's *The Burial of Sir John Moore*.

> Not a drum was heard, not a funeral note,
>   As his corpse to the rampart we hurried;
> Not a soldier discharged his farewell shot,
>   O'er the grave where our hero we buried.
>
> We buried him darkly, at dead of night,
>   The sods with our bayonets turning;
> By the struggling moonbeam's misty light
>   And the lantern dimly burning.
>   .   .   .   .
> Slowly and sadly we laid him down,
>   From the field of his fame fresh and gory;
> We carved not a line, and we raised not a stone—
>   But we left him alone with his glory.

Here we have the same *basic* metrical pattern—the anapaest—
as in Scott's poem, but the stresses fall on longer syllables and
thus it is that this poem is altogether graver and slower in tone
and in movement than *Bonny Dundee*. Notice, too, the more
frequent modulation of the basic metre. The first line of verse
two, for example, has only two trisyllabic feet, the others
being iambs; and at the end of several lines there is an extra
unstressed syllable which gives a lingering, regretful note.

> O'er the grave where our hero we buried
> But we left him alone with his glory.

Modulation is even more remarkable in the last verse where a
solemn, heavy emphasis is gained in the first line by the sudden
reversal of the metrical pattern.

Slówly ănd sádlȳ wĕ láid hĭm dówn.

Our task in this chapter is to remind ourselves of the *purpose* of rhythm in poetry. Rhythm helps to give heightened emotion, increased excitement, dignity, solemnity, light-heartedness, speed, languor, or whatever particular effect the poet is aiming at. The sole criterion that the critic should have in mind when studying the rhythm of a poem, is the effectiveness of that rhythm in sustaining its share in communicating the emotional impression which the whole poem is intended to make. That is its function.

An indifferent poet is dominated and limited by the particular metrical pattern that he is using: his verse is, in consequence, monotonous, jog-trot and mechanical. A great poet imposes the strength of his own imagining and thought on the metrical framework of his poem, varying his patterns by changes in stress, letting his lines run on, pausing here, lengthening a line there, yet always retaining the metrical *basis* of his lines and stanzas, and so securing a discipline for his work, a *form* without which there can be no great art.

Here are two examples of blank verse; the first is pre-Shakespearian, the second is from *Henry IV* (2).

[A]

> Forthwith Fame flies through the great Libyan towns:
> A mischief Fame, there is none else so swift;
> That moving grows and flitting gathers force.
> First small for dread, soon after climbs the skies;
> Stayeth on earth, and hides her head in clouds.
> Whom our mother, the earth, tempted by wrath
> Of gods, begat; the last sister (they write)
> Of Cäeus, and to Enceladus eke:
> Speedy of foot, of wing likewise as swift,
> A monster huge, and dreadful to descrive.
> In every plume that on her body sticks,
> (A thing indeed much marvellous to hear)
> As many waker eyes lurk underneath,
> So many mouths to speak, and listening ears.

By night she flies amid the cloudy sky,
Shrieking, by the dark shadow of the earth,
Ne doth decline to the sweet sleep her eyes.
By day she sits to mark on the house top,
Or turrets high; and the great towns affrays;
As mindful of ill and lies, as blasing truth.

SURREY'S TRANSLATION OF THE *Aeneid*

[B]

Rumour is a pipe
Blown by surmises, jealousies, conjectures,
And of so easy and so plain a stop
That the blunt monster with uncounted heads,
The still discordant wavering multitude,
Can play upon it. But what need I thus
My well-known body to anatomize
Among my household? Why is Rumour here?
I run before King Harry's victory;
Who in a bloody field by Shrewsbury
Hath beaten down young Hotspur and his troops,
Quenching the flame of bold rebellion
Even with the rebels' blood. But what mean I
To speak so true at first? My office is
To noise abroad that Harry Monmouth fell
Under the wrath of noble Hotspur's sword,
And that the king before the Douglas' rage
Stoop'd his anointed head as low as death.

We have chosen not to compare a piece of Shakespearian dialogue with Surrey's poetry since, to get a fair comparison, we must use passages in which both poets have a common purpose. Though Shakespeare has – characteristically – thrown his description into dramatic form, both he and Surrey are describing similar ideas, untrustworthy Fame, and Rumour.

Having read both passages aloud, you will notice at once the greater freedom of movement in B. Diagrams of the thought movement in the two passages look like this.

45

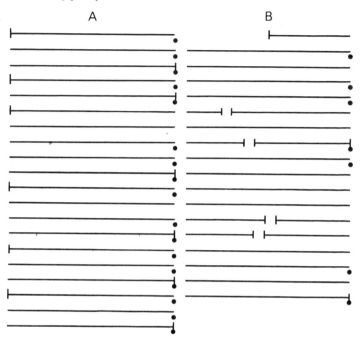

In these diagrams, the black vertical marks represent the beginning and the end of sentences; the dots indicate end-stopped lines. In the twenty lines of Surrey's poetry, seventeen are end-stopped: in Shakespeare's eighteen lines, only eight. There is a corresponding increase in rhythmic freedom in passage B where modulation of the metrical basis of the lines is the rule rather than the exception, though there is a sufficiently firm metrical framework to prevent shapelessness. For example, in this passage counterpointing is frequent, and the speech accent cuts so strongly across the metrical that a beat's rest must be taken in the middle of lines six and seven.

> Why is Rumour here?
> I run before King Harry's victory;
> Who in a bloody field by Shrewsbury
> Hath beaten down young Hotspur and his troops,

> Quenching the flame of bold rebellion
> Even with the rebels' blood. ∧ But what mean I
> To speak so true at first? ∧ My office is
> To noise abroad that Harry Monmouth fell . . .

The difference between the two passages may be summed up by saying that whereas passage A is 'line-moulded' with the thought compressed into the metrical framework, passage B is built up in thought groups which transcend and modulate the metrical basis of the lines.

A passage from *The Winter's Tale* will illustrate how far Shakespeare took this freedom in his late style.

> Is whispering nothing?
> Is leaning cheek to cheek? is meeting noses?
> Kissing with inside lip? stopping the career
> Of laughing with a sigh?—a note infallible
> Of breaking honesty—horsing foot on foot?
> Skulking in corners? wishing clocks more swift?
> Hours, minutes? noon, midnight? and all eyes
> Blind with the pin and web but theirs, theirs only,
> That would unseen be wicked? is this nothing?
> Why, then the world and all that's in't is nothing;
> The covering sky is nothing; Bohemia nothing;
> My wife is nothing; nor nothing have these nothings,
> If this be nothing.

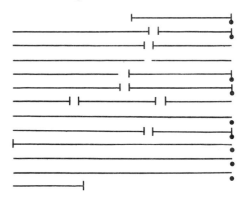

Notice the choppy, clipped utterance of the first eight and a half lines, followed by the smoother sweep of the last three and a half where Leontes, having hurled his accusations, then begs for Camillo's belief and support. This speech structure is sustained by devices such as run-on lines, feminine endings, the substitution of trochees for iambs, variations in the position of the caesura, and others, which reference to the Appendix will enable you to identify for yourself. The important thing to notice here is that while Shakespeare uses this great flexibility as a means of expressing the emotion he wished to convey – the agonised jealousy of a tortured human being – he never carries it so far that we become unconscious of the steady beat of rising duple time underlying the whole passage; a note which sustains the unity of emotion, and elevates the words above the level of everyday language even though the diction is realistic.

This passage represents the extreme limit of rhythmic flexibility. Shakespeare's successors took the process further and blank verse disintegrated into rhythmic prose; the underlying beat was lost in a welter of experiment and uncontrolled modulations of metre. Here is an extract from *Perkin Warbeck* (1634) by John Ford, which illustrates vividly the importance of form in poetry. In this passage, experiment has been carried so far, there are so many overflows, redundant syllables, and tri-syllabic feet, that the pattern of blank verse has been destroyed. This verse has no recognisable form: discipline has gone, and what should have been blank verse is merely bad prose. Inspiration should adapt the mould, it should not shatter it.

> Why peers of England,
> We'll lead 'em on courageously: I read
> A triumph over tyranny upon
> Their several foreheads. – Faint not in the moment
> Of victory! our ends, and Warwick's head,

Innocent Warwick's head,–for we are prologue
But to his tragedy,–conclude the wonder
Of Henry's fears; and then the glorious race
Of fourteen kings, Plantagenets, determines
In this last issue male; Heaven be obeyed!
Impoverish time of its amazement, friends,
And we will prove as trusty in our payments
As prodigal to nature in our debts.

This matter of the relationship between form and purpose
is fundamental to the appreciation of poetry, and we must
look at further examples. First, some non-dramatic (*ie* epic
or narrative) blank verse, taken from *Paradise Lost* (*Book I*).

Forthwith upright he rears from off the pool
His might stature; on each hand the flames
Driven backward slope their pointing spires, and, rolled
In billows, leave i' the midst a horrid vale.
Then with expanded wings he steers his flight
Aloft, incumbent on the dusky air,
That felt unusual weight; till on dry land
He lights–if it were land that ever burned
With solid, as the lake with liquid fire,
And such appeared in hue, as when the force
Of subterranean wind transports a hill
Torn from Pelorus, or the shattered side
Of thundering Etna; whose combustible
And fuelled entrails thence conceiving fire,
Sublimed with mineral fury, aid the winds,
And leave a singed bottom all involved
With stench and smoke: such resting found the sole
Of unblest feet.

Milton's purpose in this passage was very different from Shakespeare's in the extract from *The Winter's Tale* which we quoted earlier. Milton is narrating, not writing dialogue, and there is, consequently, a more even flow to the verse. The paragraphic structure is remarkable. Compare this verse-plot with those of the two Shakespearian passages, or Surrey's, and you will see that, while retaining the same metre, Milton has achieved a new structure. The jerkiness which Shakespeare used to convey Leontes' mental unrest would have been inappropriate to Milton's purpose: the more colloquial manner of the *Henry IV* passage would have been equally out of place: the cramped, line-by-line utterance of Surrey would have been inadequate to impress the reader with a sense of Satan's awful appearance and the immense horror of his doom. Milton aims at sublimity and the grand style, and expresses this in the great sweep of his lines. Modulation of the basic iambs occurs less frequently than in the passage from *The*

Winter's Tale, but there is enough counterpointing to prevent any feeling of mechanical utterance, and to delight the ear with the richly melodious effect of such lines as the following, where the metrical stress is often submerged under the compelling speech accent.

> on each hand the flames
> Driven backward slope their pointing spires, and, rolled
> In billows, leave i' the midst a horrid vale.
> Then with expanded wings he steers his flight
> Aloft, incumbent on the dusky air . . .

The linking of the second half of each of these lines with the first half of the next, sets up a kind of secondary rhythm which is supplementary to the iambic pentameters of the line units, and is powerful in creating that organ-like note for which this poet is so well renowned.

Rhyme is one of the most important 'ear-pleasing' devices of the poet. The ear is both stimulated and satisfied by a well-handled rhyme-scheme as the various consonant and vowel combinations are caught up and re-echoed. What we should notice at once is that mere rhyming is not enough to give satisfaction. There is nothing technically wrong with the rhymes in the following verse, yet the comic banality of what was meant to be a serious lament arises as much from the too-obvious rhymes as from the monotonous jog-trot of the iambics and the pedestrian diction.

> They cheerfulness remembered still
> And with us as in days of yore,
> Not lost, but merely gone before;
> Forget thee, no we never will!

It is quite clear that this 'poetry' has been built round the rhymes. Look, for example, at the last line where the natural order of the words–'we will never forget thee'–has been

wrenched violently to force 'will' to the end of the line, and so
secure the rhyme with 'still'. When the form of poetry masters
the thought and emotion, doggerel results. Here, for contrast,
is a stanza from Tennyson's *In Memoriam*, written in exactly
the same metre, and having exactly the same rhyme-scheme.
In this, however, the thought and emotion use the form of
the verse as their vehicle, and we are conscious of the versification merely as one of the means whereby the poet achieves
his end.

> Thy voice is on the rolling air;
> I hear thee where the waters run;
> Thou standest in the rising sun
> And in the setting thou art fair.

The use made of rhyme will depend upon the poet's
purposes. It should be in harmony with the versification as a
whole, just as the latter should reinforce and enrich the
imagery and the theme. (See Chapter 5, especially pp.
111–113.)

Pope's 'Essay on Man' provides good illustrations of the
epigrammatic effect of couplets.

> Order is Heaven's first law; and this confess'd,
> Some are, and must be, greater than the rest,
> More rich, more wise; but who infers from hence
> That such are happier, shocks all commonsense.

Pope intended his words to be memorable, and the closeness
of the rhymes is conducive to this: he meant to express truths
pithily and pointedly; the swift, clear rhymes clinch his arguments. It is difficult indeed to dissent from propositions so
urbanely advanced, and so easily and pleasantly read. To that
urbanity, ease and pleasure, the rhyme-scheme and the quality
of the rhymes contribute much.

> For forms of government let fools contest:
> Whate'er is best administer'd is best:

For modes of faith, let graceless zealots fight;
His can't be wrong whose life is in the right;
In faith and hope the world will disagree,
But all mankind's concern is charity:
All must be false that thwart this one great end:
And all of God that bless mankind or mend.

The couplet is used for much the same purpose at the end of a Shakespearian (Elizabethan or English) sonnet.

When I do count the clock that tells the time,
And see the brave day sunk in hideous night;
When I behold the violet past prime,
And sable curls all silver'd o'er with white;
When lofty trees I see barren of leaves,
Which erst from heat did canopy the herd,
And summer's green all girded up in sheaves,
Borne on the bier with white and bristly beard,
Then of thy beauty do I question make,
That thou among the wastes of time must go,
Since sweets and beauties do themselves forsake
And dies as fast as they see others grow;
  And nothing gainst Time's scythe can make defence
  Save breed, to brave him when he takes thee hence.

The theme here is mortality and the first twelve lines build up a powerful impression of the brevity of beauty and of life. The rhymes divide these twelve lines into three quatrains, each of which contains a distinct section of the theme and yet is linked with the others by the essential continuity of thought and emotion running through all three. The last two lines, however, introduce a distinctly new turn of thought; there is, after all, one way of defeating time—in one's children one achieves immortality. This thought is expressed in a couplet, and the sudden chiming of the new rhyme gives a triumphant clinch to the idea. The pattern of the whole poem is

4–4–4–2.

The Petrarchan sonnet is built on a completely different plan and it is its rhyme-scheme that marks it off so distinctly from the Shakespearian sonnet since in length and number of lines, and in metre, the two are identical.

Wordsworth's sonnet 'Milton' is a fine example of the Petrarchan form.

> Milton, thou shouldst be living at this hour:
> England hath need of thee: she is a fen
> Of stagnant waters: altar, sword, and pen,
> Fireside, the heroic wealth of hall and bower,
> Have forfeited their ancient English dower
> Of inward happiness. We are selfish men;
> Oh! raise us up, return to us again;
> And give us manners, virtue, freedom, power.
> Thy soul was like a Star, and dwelt apart:
> Thou hadst a voice whose sound was like the sea:
> Pure as the naked heavens, majestic, free,
> So didst thou travel on life's common way,
> In cheerful godliness; and yet thy heart
> The lowliest duties on herself did lay.

The pattern here is 8–6 and the poem is built up on two distinct waves of emotion. The first wave is expressed in the octave or octet (the first eight lines); the second fills the next six (the sestet). In a Shakespearian sonnet the turning point of the poem is held off until the end of the twelfth line; in the Petrarchan sonnet it comes at the end of the eighth. Frequently, the position of the pause between octave and sestet is varied, sometimes coming as late as the middle of the ninth line, or even at the beginning of the tenth. If it comes later than this, however, it gravely weakens the force of the sestet; and it should never come earlier than the end of the eighth line, or the power of the octave to develop the first part of the theme is destroyed. The rhyme-scheme of the octave is always a–b–b–a–a–b–b–a. This firmness and closeness of rhyme gives a unity of tone to the first eight lines which assists in developing firmly the statement of the theme. But it is in the sestet that the full melody of sonnet-rhyme is heard. In the sonnet we have just quoted, the sestet rhyme-scheme is c–d–d–e–c–e, but c–d–c–d–c–d, or c–d–e–c–d–e, or any variation of these, is commonly found. This wider spacing of the rhymes avoids any suggestion of a jingle, yet the rhymes are just sufficiently pronounced to satisfy the ear. The sestet of a Petrarchan sonnet should never end with a couplet – this is the unique mark of a Shakespearian sonnet, and would be unsuitable to the Petrarchan which already has three close rhymes in the octave.

In his sonnets, Milton often omits the octave-sestet pause altogether, so that many critics distinguish a third kind of sonnet, the Miltonic. Even when he avoids the break in theme, however, he changes his rhyme-scheme in the sestet, and so achieves a new melody in the second half of his sonnets, just as is found in the Petrarchan form proper.

ON THE LATE MASSACRE IN PIEDMONT

> Avenge, O Lord, thy slaughter'd saints, whose bones
> Lie scatter'd on the Alpine mountains cold;
> Ev'n them who kept thy truth so pure of old,
> When all our fathers worshipp'd stocks and stones,
> Forget not: in thy book record their groans
> Who were thy sheep, and in their ancient fold
> Slain by the bloody Piedmontese that roll'd
> Mother with infant down the rocks. Their moans
> The vales redoubled to the hills, and they
> To Heav'n. Their martyr'd blood and ashes sow
> O'er all the Italian fields, where still doth sway
> The triple tyrant; that from these may grow
> A hundred fold, who having learn'd thy way
> Early may fly the Babylonian woe.

In this sonnet, the octave-sestet turn is present but is held off until the beginning of the tenth line, leaving Milton with just sufficient space for the utterance of his powerful second wave of emotion.

The second danger of the Shakespearian sonnet is that the

final couplet may easily degenerate from a chime to a jingle. Shakespeare, himself, did not always avoid this; and Keats, who wrote many magnificent sonnets, was nevertheless capable of perpetrating the abominable rhymes of this sonnet: 'Written at the end of *The Floure and the Lefe*.'

> This pleasant tale is like a little copse:
>   The honied lines do freshly interlace
>   To keep the reader in so sweet a place,
> So that he here and there full-hearted stops;
> And oftentimes he feels the dewy drops
>   Come cool and suddenly against his face,
>   And by the wandering melody may trace
> Which way the tender-legged linnet hops.
> Oh! what a power hath white Simplicity!
>   What mighty power has this gentle story!
>   I that for ever feel athirst for glory!
> Could at this moment be content to lie
>   Meekly upon the grass, as one whose sobbings
>   Were heard of none beside the mournful robbins.

The execrable rhyme at the end is an extreme case, but double rhymes are usually to be avoided in the sonnet; they are too unwieldy for its delicate music. Notice too how the poem is weakened by the lack of proper variety of rhyme in the sestet – quite apart from the fact that they are very bad rhymes. Of course, this sonnet is neither strictly Shakespearian, nor truly Petrarchan in structure. It has an octave-sestet pause and the octave rhymes in the Petrarchan manner, but the sestet begins with a quadruple rhyme and ends with a double-rhymed couplet. A singularly unpleasing arrangement.

Our example from Pope illustrated the epigrammatic effect of couplets. In Goldsmith's *Deserted Village*, however, they are used for a different purpose. The quiet, even flow of description and reflection is carried smoothly along by the melodious rhymes which are generally made on longer syllables than those employed by Pope for his rhyming words.

Sweet Auburn! parent of the blissful hour,
Thy glades forlorn confess the tyrant power.
Here, as I take my solitary rounds
Amidst thy tangled walks and ruined grounds,
And, many a year elapsed, return to view
Where once the cottage stood, the hawthorn grew,
Remembrance wakes with all her busy train,
Swells at my breast, and turns the past to pain.
    In all my wanderings round this world of care,
In all my griefs – and God has given my share –
I still had hopes, my latest hours to crown,
Amidst these humble bowers to lay me down;
To husband out life's taper at the close,
And keep the flame from wasting by repose.

Clearly, the close vowels and hissing consonants of the rhymes in this next extract, which comes from Pope's *Prologue To The Satires* (*Epistle To Dr Arbuthnot*) and is a scathing attack on his literary rivals and enemies, would have been out of place in Goldsmith's gentle lines.

Pains, reading, study, are their just pretence,
And all they want is spirit, taste, and sense.
Commas and points they set exactly right,
And 'twere a sin to rob them of their mite;
Yet ne'er one sprig of laurel graced these ribalds,
From slashing Bentley down to piddling Tibbalds:
Each wight, who reads not, and but scans and spells,
Each word-catcher that lives on syllables.
Even such small critics, some regard may claim,
Preserved in Milton's or in Shakespeare's name.
Pretty! in amber to observe such forms
Of hairs, or straws, or dirt, or grubs, or worms!

Compare this again with Johnson's general satire on human life in *The Vanity of Human Wishes*, where the rhymes sustain the broader theme with full, portentous sounds.

The festal blazes, the triumphal show,
The ravish'd standard, and the captive foe,
The senate's thanks, the gazette's pompous tale,
With force resistless o'er the brave prevail.
Such bribes the rapid Greek o'er Asia whirl'd,
For such the steady Romans shook the world;
For such in distant lands the Britons shine,
And stain with blood the Danube or the Rhine;
This pow'r has praise, that virtue scarce can warm,
Till fame supplies the universal charm.
Yet Reason frowns on War's unequal game,
Where wasted nations raise a single name,
And mortgaged states their grandsires' wreaths regret,
From age to age in everlasting debt;
Wreaths which at last the dear-bought right convey
To rust on medals, or on stones decay.

An extract from *Marmion* gives a vivid illustration of the interplay of sense, rhyme and rhythm.

But as they left the dark'ning heath,
More desperate grew the strife of death.
The English shafts in volleys hail'd,
In headlong charge their horse assail'd;
Front, flank and rear, the squadrons sweep,
To break the Scottish circle deep,
    That fought around their king.
But yet, though thick the shafts as snow,
Though charging knights like whirlwinds go,
Though bill-men ply the ghastly blow,
    Unbroken was the ring.

These lines are shorter than those used in heroic couplets and more suitable to sustain the speed of action-narrative. The quick couplet rhymes hurry the verse along until line seven – which is one foot shorter than its predecessors – brings a pause in the energetic sweep of the story. Then comes the bunching of rhymes in the triplet before the second short line, so building up a sense of expectancy which is fully satisfied by the climax achieved when this rhymes with the previous trimeter.

A more intricate rhyme-pattern is seen in Arnold's 'Thyrsis' where the subtle and haunting music of the verses depends very largely on the rhymes.

> So, some tempestuous morn in early June,
>> When the year's primal burst of bloom is o'er,
>>> Before the roses and the longest day—
>> When the garden-walks and all the grassy floor
>> With blossoms red and white of fallen May
> And chestnut-flowers are strewn—
>> So have I heard the cuckoo's parting cry,
>>> From the wet field, through the vext garden-trees,
>>> Come with the volleying rain and tossing breeze:
>> 'The bloom is gone, and with the bloom go I!'

You will see how rhyme is held off until the end of the fourth line so that the ear has almost ceased to expect it. Then comes the first rhyme; another in the next line; while the sixth line reaches right back to the first to echo its final sound. In the last four lines, rhyme is constant and swift, contrasting vividly with the slower rhymes of the earlier lines. The long silences of the first six lines are replaced by the quickly recurring harmonies of the last four. Notice, too, the rest afforded by line six; the counterpointing in lines seven, eight, and nine; and the superb effect of interposing the couplet between lines seven and ten.

It is interesting to compare with the structure of Arnold's lament, the form of these lines, also on the subject of death. You will learn much about form and rhyme quality from such a comparison.

> Ah, tell me not that life goes on,
>> That Death is short, the grave a bed,
> That holds us brief in twilight wan
>> When on Death's couch we lay our head.

> For he was here and leapt and sang;
>   The arrow flew; the singer failed:
> Death's iron portal's icy clang
>   Hath severed us from him we hailed.
>   We shall not meet in sweet, dim gloamings
>   For all our prayers and tears and moanings,
>   This is the end of all our rovings:
>   The bark hath weighed and sailed.

The Spenserian stanza is one of the most melodious forms that English poetry has used. Here is an example:

> Then came the Autumn all in yellow clad,
> As though he joyed in his plenteous store,
> Laden with fruits that made him laugh, full glad
> That he had banisht hunger, which to-fore
> Had by the belly oft him pinched sore.
> Upon his head a wreath that was enrold
> With ears of corn, of every sort he bore:
> And in his hand a sickle he did hold,
> To reap the ripened fruits the which the earth had yold.

Read the verse aloud and then answer these questions which are designed to enable you to discover for yourself the secret of its charm.

1 What is the rhythm? How does the last line differ from the others, and what is its effect?
2 What is the rhyme-scheme?
3 How many rhymes are there, and what would be lost by increasing the number of rhymes?

The following verse is a more modern example of this stanza. By studying it carefully you will be led to a clear understanding of the beauty of form that it offers to the poet who can use it.

> There have been tears and breaking hearts for thee,
> And mine were nothing, had I such to give;
> But when I stood beneath the fresh green tree,
> Which living waves where thou didst cease to live,

And saw around me the wide field revive
With fruits and fertile promise, and the Spring
Come forth her work of gladness to contrive,
With all her reckless birds upon the wing,
I turn'd from all she brought to those she could not bring.

Your study of that verse of Byron's should proceed on these lines (as, indeed, should your study of all poetic form): What is the poet trying to do? How does the form that he is using aid him in his task?

The stanza used by Coleridge in 'Christabel' is of great interest. In this poem the length of the verses and of the lines varies frequently, but the rhythmical basis of each line is constant – four accented syllables to the line. The total number of syllables in each line varies, however, from as few as seven, to as many as twelve, because the number of *unaccented* syllables is continually changing.

Outside her kennel, the mastiff old
Lay fast asleep, in moonshine cold.
The mastiff old did not awake,
Yet she an angry moan did make.
And what can ail the mastiff bitch?
Never till now she uttered yell
Beneath the eye of Christabel.
Perhaps it is the owlet's scritch:
For what can ail the mastiff bitch?

or again,

The night is chill; the forest bare;
Is it the wind that moaneth bleak?
There is not wind enough in the air
To move away the ringlet curl
From the lovely lady's cheek –
There is not wind enough to twirl

> The one red leaf, the last of its clan,
> That dances as often as dance it can
> Hanging so light and hanging so high,
> On the topmost twig that looks up at the sky.

The melody that Coleridge created here is peculiarly fitting in its flexibility and subtlety to the atmosphere of the supernatural story that he is telling. Notice, for example, the gradual shift from duple to triple time that takes place in the above lines. His use of *accents instead of feet as the basis of his rhythm* is an important anticipation of much modern prosody, a development that we must now discuss.

There is no need to be put off by the apparent difficulty of much modern verse; what is required from the reader is that sympathetic and imaginative approach without which no poetry – whether 'traditional' or 'modern' – can be enjoyed. We have already referred to the necessity of clearing our minds of prejudice when confronted with the vocabulary of the modern poet, and we shall turn to similar problems in the chapters on diction and imagery; here, we need deal only with modern versification.

The most important development in modern prosody was the use of 'Sprung Rhythm' by Gerard Manley Hopkins. Hopkins was, chronologically speaking, a Victorian (1844–89), but in its spirit of ceaseless experiment his poetry belongs wholly to the modern age. He was anxious to seek out new methods of expression and, though his versification was in some ways a return to the metrical principles of 'Piers Plowman', he so successfully captured the imagination of his successors, that a 'new' prosody was born. The basis of sprung rhythm is similar to that of the 'Christabel' stanza since the 'value' of each line depends not on the number of its feet, but of its accents; the difference being that while Coleridge never associated more than two unaccented syllables with each of his stresses, Hopkins allowed three and more slack syllables to each accented one, and permitted two, three, or more accented syllables to come together. His striking use of alliteration (see, too, 'Piers Plowman' and pre-Chaucerian alliterative verse) supplies a bold pattern in place of the metrical pattern which he abandons. Here is an example of sprung rhythm from 'Felix Randal'.

> How far from then forethought of, all thy more boisterous
> years,
> When thou at the random grim forge, powerful amidst
> peers,
> Didst fettle for the great grey drayhorse his bright and
> battering sandal.

If these lines are read aloud, letting the voice clearly stress the syllables that naturally demand emphasis, it will be found that the versification of sprung rhythm is no more 'difficult' than that of 'Christabel'. The test for the critic is the same here as everywhere: does the versification advance or hinder the poet's purpose?

Many modern poets have been influenced by Hopkins' versification, and sprung rhythm and free verse are common poetic forms today. Free verse, which owes much to Walt Whitman, does not make use of patterns of alliteration, but is similar to sprung rhythm in its use of accent. In free verse, the poet abandons the steady beat of a regular rhythmic pattern with its constancy and its variations, substituting for this, lines grouped in emotional rather than rhythmic units. But here, no less than in traditional measures, stress and quantity are of enormous importance in the transmission of feeling and thought. A brief extract from *The Waste Land* will help to establish this point and to demonstrate the metrical kinship of free verse and sprung rhythm.

> The river's tent is broken: the last fingers of leaf
> Clutch and sink into the wet bank. The wind
> Crosses the brown land, unheard. The nymphs are
> departed.

On the other hand, your ear will tell you that those lines also have a rhythmic affinity with blank verse. Eliot – one of the great exponents of 'free verse' in the twentieth century – was always deeply influenced by traditional measures. His verse constantly moves near to, then away from, the pattern of the iambic pentameter. 'Counting' of stressed syllables and feet will not discover a 'regular' metric; but beneath all the other effects is a recurring iambic beat.

'Modern' poets tried to break away from the style that they had inherited from the nineteenth century, but this was not revolt for revolt's sake. As we have seen already, the great poets have always modified verse forms to express their own individual visions. It was because the post-1900 poets felt that 'orthodox' patterns and accepted 'poetic' diction had stifled their immediate predecessors that they broke dramatically with inherited traditions. Yet they were keenly aware of their poetic inheritance and, as in Eliot's case, more concerned to re-vitalise that inheritance than to pretend that it did not exist. Determined not to be dominated by an accepted style, their bold experiments yet showed an understanding of its methods and conventions.

Free verse, which played a dominant part in English poetry from about 1914 to about 1945, evolved in the belief that a poem grows out of the experience that gives it birth. Rhythm was used to express intention, tone and mood, shifting flexibly as the poetic statement of the experience developed. A set pattern was avoided because it seemed to impose arbitrary rules on the poet, but all the elements that made up the patterns of the past – rhyme, half-rhyme, alliteration, assonance, regular metres – were employed from time to time.

If carefully analysed, the following poems make those points clear. Each is representative of work that dominated poetic theory and practice up to the end of the second world war. Not every poem quoted is 'revolutionary' in metrical technique, but close study of them all will illustrate how flexible versification can be while yet providing an appropriate form within which ideas and emotions are caught.

Bear in mind as you read them Ezra Pound's statement: 'Poetry is a composition of words set to music. . . . The proportion . . . of the music may, and does, vary . . . but poetry withers and "dries out" when it leaves music . . . too far behind it.'

INVERSNAID

This darksome burn, horseback brown,
His rollrock highroad roaring down,
In coop and in comb the fleece of his foam
Flutes and low to the lake falls home.

A windpuff-bonnet of fawn-froth
Turns and twindles over the broth
Of a pool so pitchblack féll-frówning,
It rounds and rounds Despair to drowning.

Degged with dew, dappled with dew
Are the groins of the braes that the brook treads through,
Wiry heathpacks, flitches of fern,
And the beadbonny ash that sits over the burn.

What would the world be, once bereft
Of wet and of wildness? Let them be left,
O let them be left, wildness and wet;
Long live the weeds and the wilderness yet.

GERARD MANLEY HOPKINS

(From) THE WRECK OF THE DEUTSCHLAND

I am soft sift
In an hourglass—at the wall
Fast, but mined with a motion, a drift,
And it crowds and it combs to the fall;
I steady as a water in a well, to a poise, to a pane,
But roped with, always, all the way down from the tall
Fells or flanks of the voel, a vein
Of the gospel proffer, a pressure, a principle, Christ's gift.

GERARD MANLEY HOPKINS

65

ARMS AND THE BOY

Let the boy try along this bayonet-blade
How cold steel is, and keen with hunger of blood;
Blue with all malice, like a madman's flash;
And thinly drawn with famishing for flesh.

Lend him to stroke these blind, blunt bullet-heads
Which long to nuzzle in the hearts of lads,
Or give him cartridges of fine zinc teeth,
Sharp with the sharpness of grief and death.

For his teeth seem for laughing round an apple.
There lurk no claws behind his fingers supple;
And god will grow no talons at his heels,
Nor antlers through the thickness of his curls.

WILFRED OWEN

(From) LITTLE GIDDING

What we call the beginning is often the end
And to make an end is to make a beginning.
The end is where we start from. And every phrase
And sentence that is right (where every word is at home,
Taking its place to support the others,
The word neither diffident nor ostentatious,
An easy commerce of the old and the new,
The common word exact without vulgarity,
The formal word precise but not pedantic,
The complete consort dancing together)
Every phrase and every sentence is an end and a beginning,
Every poem an epitaph. And any action
Is a step to the block, to the fire, down the sea's throat
Or to an illegible stone: and that is where we start.
We die with the dying:
See, they depart, and we go with them.
We are born with the dead:
See, they return and bring us with them.
The moment of the rose and the moment of the yew-tree
Are of equal duration. A people without history

Is not redeemed from time, for history is a pattern
Of timeless moments. So, while the light fails
On a winter's afternoon, in a secluded chapel
History is now and England.

T. S. ELIOT

HUMMING-BIRD

I can imagine, in some otherworld
Primeval-dumb, far back
In that most awful stillness, that only gasped and hummed,
Humming-birds raced down the avenues.

Before anything had a soul,
While life was a heave of Matter, half inanimate,
This little bit chipped off in brilliance
And went whizzing through the slow, vast, succulent stems.

I believe there were no flowers then,
In the world where the humming-bird flashed ahead of creation.
I believe he pierced the slow vegetable veins with his long beak.

Probably he was big
As mosses, and little lizards, they say, were once big.
Probably he was a jabbing, terrifying monster.

We look at him through the wrong end of the long telescope
of Time

Luckily for us.

D. H LAWRENCE

Versification is an auxiliary, a subtle ally of the poet, helping him by its music to arouse in the reader emotions similar to those that stirred him as he wrote. The first appeal of poetry is to the ear, and versification is one of the means whereby beauty of sound is achieved. If the ear is pleased, the critical mind will naturally enquire into the sources of its pleasure. It is then that we examine the versification closely, and only then that we are wholly conscious of the craftsmanship that went into its making. To that craftsmanship and to its product we may

67

apply with peculiar fitness the observation which Coleridge in *Biographia Literaria* made in a wider connexion: 'Nothing can permanently please which does not contain the reason within itself why it is so and not otherwise.'

PRACTICAL WORK

1

What is the poet's intention in each of the following passages, and how far does the versification (*ie* rhythm, rhyme-scheme, stanza-form, *etc*) help or hinder that purpose? (N.B. In this exercise the passages are grouped in such a way as to draw your attention to the differences in style that different purposes impose on poems sharing a common metrical basis.)

[A]

> Peace to all such! but were there one whose fires
> True genius kindles, and fair fame inspires;
> Blest with each talent, and each art to please,
> And born to write, converse, and live with ease;
> Should such a man, too fond to rule alone,
> Bear, like the Turk, no brother near the throne,
> View him with scornful, yet with jealous eyes,
> And hate for arts that caused himself to rise;
> Damn with faint praise, assent with civil leer,
> And, without sneering, teach the rest to sneer;
> Willing to wound, and yet afraid to strike,
> Just hint a fault, and hesitate dislike;
> Alike reserved to blame, or to commend,
> A timorous foe, and a suspicious friend;
> Dreading e'en fools, by flatterers besieged,
> And so obliging, that he ne'er obliged;
> Like Cato, give his little senate laws,
> And sit attentive to his own applause;
> While wits and Templars every sentence raise,
> And wonder with a foolish face of praise—
> Who but must laugh, if such a man there be?
> Who would not weep, if Atticus were he?

[B]

Beside yon straggling fence that skirts the way,
With blossomed furze unprofitably gay,
There, in his noisy mansion, skilled to rule,
The village master taught his little school.
A man severe he was, and stern to view;
I knew him well, and every truant knew:
Well had the boding tremblers learned to trace
The day's disasters in his morning face;
Full well they laughed with counterfeited glee
At all his jokes, for many a joke had he;
Full well the busy whisper circling round
Conveyed the dismal tidings when he frowned.
Yet he was kind, or, if severe in aught,
The love he bore to learning was in fault;
The village all declared how much he knew:
'Twas certain he could write, and cipher too;
Lands he could measure, terms and tides presage,
And e'en the story ran that he could gauge:
In arguing, too, the parson owned his skill;
For e'en though vanquished, he could argue still;
While words of learned length and thundering sound
Amazed the gazing rustics ranged around;
And still they gazed, and still the wonder grew
That one small head could carry all he knew.

[C]

By numbers here from shame or censure free,
All crimes are safe, but hated poverty.
This, only this, the rigid law pursues,
This, only this, provokes the snarling muse.
The sober trader at a tatter'd cloak,
Wakes from his dream, and labours for a joke;
With brisker air the silken courtiers gaze,
And turn the varied taunt a thousand ways.
Of all the griefs that harass the distress'd,
Sure the most bitter is a scornful jest;
Fate never wounds more deep the gen'rous heart,
Than when a blockhead's insult points the dart.
   Has heaven reserved, in pity to the poor,

No pathless waste, or undiscover'd shore?
No secret island in the boundless main?
No peaceful desert yet unclaim'd by Spain?
Quick let us rise, the happy seats explore,
And bear oppression's insolence no more.
This mournful truth is ev'rywhere confess'd,
SLOW RISES WORTH, BY POVERTY DEPRESS'D:
But here more slow, where all are slaves to gold,
Where looks are merchandise, and smiles are sold;
Where won by bribes, by flatteries implor'd,
The groom retails the favours of his lord.

[D]

Time hath, my lord, a wallet at his back,
Wherein he puts alms for oblivion,
A great-sized monster of ingratitudes:
Those scraps are good deeds past; which are devour'd
As fast as they are made, forgot as soon
As done: perseverance, dear my lord,
Keeps honour bright: to have done is to hang
Quite out of fashion, like a rusty mail
In monumental mockery. Take the instant way;
For honour travels in a strait so narrow,
Where one but goes abreast.

[E]

The night was winter in his roughest mood,
The morning sharp and clear. But now at noon,
Upon the southern side of the slant hills,
And where the woods fence off the northern blast,
The season smiles, resigning all its rage,
And has the warmth of May. The vault is blue
Without a cloud, and white without a speck,
The dazzling splendour of the scene below.
Again the harmony comes o'er the vale,
And through the trees I view the embattled tower
Whence all the music. I again perceive
The soothing influence of the wafted strains,
And settle in soft musings as I tread
The walk, still verdant, under oaks and elms,
Whose outspread branches overarch the glade.

[F]

Look here, upon this picture, and on this,
The counterfeit presentment of two brothers.
See what a grace was seated on this brow;
Hyperion's curls, the front of Jove himself,
An eye like Mars, to threaten and command;
A station like the herald Mercury
New-lighted on a heaven-kissing hill;
A combination and a form indeed,
Where every god did seem to set his seal
To give the world assurance of a man:
This was your husband. Look you now, what follows:
Here is your husband; like a mildew'd ear,
Blasting his wholesome brother. Have you eyes?
Could you on this fair mountain leave to feed,
And batten on this moor? Ha! have you eyes?
You cannot call it love, for at your age
The hey-day in the blood is tame, it's humble,
And waits upon the judgement; and what judgement
Would step from this to this?

[G]

Much have I travell'd in the realms of gold,
    And many goodly states and kingdoms seen;
    Round many western islands have I been
Which bards in fealty to Apollo hold.
Oft of one wide expanse had I been told
    That deep-brow'd Homer ruled as his demesne;
    Yet did I never breathe its pure serene
Till I heard Chapman speak out loud and bold:
Then felt I like some watcher of the skies
    When a new planet swims into his ken;
Or like stout Cortez when with eagle eyes
    He star'd at the Pacific—and all his men
Look'd at each other in a wild surmise—
    Silent, upon a peak in Darien.

[H]

Leave me, O Love, which reachest but to dust;
And thou my mind, aspire to higher things;

71

Grow rich in that which never taketh rust;
Whatever fades, but fading pleasures brings,
Draw in thy beams, and humble all thy might
To that sweet yoke, where lasting freedoms be;
Which breaks the clouds, and opens forth the light
That doth both shine and give us sight to see.
O take fast hold; let that light be thy guide
In this small course which birth draws out to death,
And think how evil becometh him to slide,
Who seeketh heaven and comes of heavenly breath.
Then farewell, world; thy uttermost I see:
Eternal Love, maintain thy Life in me.

2

The five passages in this exercise illustrate the use of five
different metres. Discuss the qualities of each.

[A]

Remote, unfriended, melancholy, slow,
Or by the lazy Scheld or wandering Po;
Or onward where the rude Carinthian boor
Against the homeless stranger shuts the door;
Or where Campania's plain forsaken lies,
A weary waste expanding to the skies,
Where'er I roam, whatever realms I see,
My heart untravelled fondly turns to thee,
Still to my brother turns, with ceaseless pain,
And drags at each remove a lengthening chain.

[B]

Comrades, leave me here a little, while as yet 'tis early morn:
Leave me here, and when you want me, sound upon the bugle
    horn.
'Tis the place, and all around it, as of old, the curlews call,
Dreary gleams about the moorland flying over Locksley Hall;
Locksley Hall, that in the distance overlooks the sandy tracts,
And the hollow ocean-ridges roaring into cataracts.

[c]

The Assyrian came down like the wolf on the fold,
And his cohorts were gleaming in purple and gold;
And the sheen of their spears was like stars on the sea,
When the blue wave rolls nightly on deep Galilee.

[d]

Just for a handful of silver he left us,
    Just for a riband to stick in his coat—
Found the one gift of which fortune bereft us,
    Lost all the others she lets us devote;
They, with the gold to give, doled him out silver,
    So much was theirs who so little allowed:
How all our copper had gone for his service!
    Rags—were they purple, his heart had been proud.

[e]

I caught this morning morning's minion, kingdom of
    daylight's dauphin, dapple-dawn-drawn
    Falcon, in his riding
Of the rolling level underneath him steady air, and striding
High there, how he rung upon the rein of a wimpling wing
In his ecstasy! then off, off forth on swing,
    As a skate's heel sweeps smooth on a bow-bend: the hurl
        and gliding
    Rebuffed the big wind. My heart in hiding
Stirred for a bird,—the achieve of, the mastery of the thing!

3

Comment on the versification of the following passages,
noticing particularly the interplay of sound and sense, of stress
and quantity, and any use of counterpointing.

[a]

I am two fooles, I know,
For loving and for saying so
    In whining Poëtry.
But where's that wiseman, that would not be I,
    If she would not deny?
Then as th' earth's inward narrow crooked lanes

Do purge sea waters fretfull salt away,
   I thought, if I could draw my paines,
Through Rimes vexation, I should them allay,
Grief brought to numbers cannot be so fierce,
For, he tames it, that fetters it in verse.

[B]

Let not thy divining heart
   Forethinke me any ill,
Destiny may take thy part,
   And may thy feares fulfill;
     But thinke that wee
Are but turn'd aside to sleepe;
They who one another keepe
   Alive, ne'r parted bee.

[C]

Fame's pillar here at last we set,
Outduring marble, brass or jet:
   Charm'd and enchanted so
   As to withstand the blow
     Of over throw:
     Nor shall the seas,
     Or outrages
     Of storms o'erbear
     What we up-rear:
     Tho' Kingdoms fall,
   This pillar never shall
   Decline or waste at all;
But stand forever by his own
Firm and well-fixed foundation.

[D]

Oh! talk not to me of a name great in story;
The days of our youth are the days of our glory;
And the myrtle and ivy of sweet two-and-twenty
Are worth all your laurels though ever so plenty.

What are garlands and crowns to the brow that is wrinkled?
'Tis but as a dead flower with May-dew be-sprinkled.
Then away with all such from the head that is hoary!
What care I for the wreaths that can only give glory!

[E]

The rock shone bright, the kirk no less,
That stands above the rock:
The moonlight steeped in silentness
The steady weathercock.
And the bay was white with silent night,
Till rising from the same,
Full many shapes that shadows were,
In crimson colours came.

[F]

The rain had fallen, the Poet arose,
　He passed by the town and out of the street,
A light wind blew from the gates of the Sun,
　And waves of shadow went over the wheat,
And he sat him down in a lonely place,
　And chanted a melody loud and sweet,
That made the wild-swan pause in her cloud,
　And the lark drop down at his feet.

[G]

The country's charms
Are hedgerows thick,
And hill-top farms,
And the fat hayrick.
Fields thick with clover,
Skies white over,
With fleecy clouds
Like giants' shrouds.
Peace comes at nightfall,
Hearing the light call
Of cooing, amorous doves.
The sun in a silver sky
Sends forth a last goodbye,
And leaves all the world to its loves.

[H]

A country life is sweet;
　In moderate cold and heat,
To walk in the air how pleasant and fair,
　In every field of wheat,

The fairest of flowers adorning the bowers,
    And every meadow's brow;
So that, I say, no courtier may
Compare with they who clothe in grey,
    And follow the useful plough.

They rise with the morning lark,
    And labour till almost dark,
Then folding their sheep, they hasten to sleep;
    While every pleasant park
Next morning is ringing with birds that are singing
    On each green, tender bough.
With what content and merriment
Their days are spent, whose minds are bent
    To follow the useful plough!

[1]

Listen, listen, Mary mine,
To the whisper of the Apennine,
It bursts on the roof like the thunder's roar,
Or like the sea on a northern shore,
Heard in its raging ebb and flow
By the captives pent in the cave below.
The Apennine in the light of day
Is a mighty mountain dim and gray,
Which between the earth and sky doth lay;
But when night comes, a chaos dread
On the dim starlight then is spread,
And the Apennine walks abroad with the storm.

4
Style: Diction

We cannot better begin an investigation of words and phrases in poetry than by calling to mind Coleridge's statement: 'Whatever lines (in poetry) can be translated into other words of the same language, without diminution of their significance . . . are so far vicious in their diction.' This 'untranslatableness' is our major test of the diction employed by poets. Poetry is much more compressed and intense than prose, and so demands a highly imaginative use of language if the feelings aroused in the reader are to be those which excited the poet as he wrote. Great poetry cannot be made with words loosely and unthoughtfully applied to the scenes, incidents or emotions that they are supposed to be communicating; rather, it arouses in the reader an overwhelming sense that the words chosen are the *right* ones for the work in hand, and that no others could possibly be used in that context without altering for the worse both the total impression made by the poem, and the meaning of the line in which substitution has occurred. Test this for yourself by considering the following passages.

[A]

> Now the golden morn aloft
>   Waves her dew-bespangled wing,
> With vermil cheek, and whisper soft
>   She woos the tardy Spring.

If the adjectives in those lines are examined carefully, it will be found that many of them are loosely applied, and that substitutes could be found for them without damaging each separate description, or reducing the total impression made by the lines.

[B]

> Or, if chill blustering winds, or driving rain,
> Prevent my willing feet, be mine the hut,
>   That from the mountain's side,
>   Views wilds, and swelling floods,
> And hamlets brown, and dim-discovered spires;
> And hears their simple bell, and marks o'er all
>   Thy dewy fingers draw
>   The gradual dusky veil.

Here, on the other hand, the adjectives are both precise and suggestive. Try, for example, to substitute another adjective for 'dim-discovered', and you will find that any other reduces the impact which the line makes on the visual sense and on the imagination. In using 'dim-discovered' to describe 'spires', the poet was relying on sense perceptions stored in the memory of his readers. Note how an almost physical sense of gazing through rain across an often obscured landscape is caught by this adjective, which, coupled with 'spires', so exactly suggests the faint appearance of distant churches, now glimpsed, now lost in the squalls.

It is inevitable that this test of the absolute rightness of the diction should be applied to poetry, since in writing a poem, the main aim is to employ such words in such an order as will evoke in an imaginative reader a response as exactly as possible harmonious with the experience which filled the poet's mind as he wrote, and which he felt to be valuable. Clearly then, a poet must be unceasing in his search for the right words. But to choose the right words in poetry is a much more difficult task than in prose, for the poet is usually working in an atmosphere of high emotional tension. One false word may destroy the whole effect that he was aiming at, just as the employment of the wrong chemical might explode an unstable mixture in a laboratory. Every significant word in every line of a poem is charged with emotion; before a new word can be added, the poet must ask himself, not merely, is this the right word for the immediate task in hand? but also, and just as importantly, is this word suitable for its context? will it harmonise with, and reinforce the effect of the words I have already used, or will it produce friction and a violent dispersal of the emotional atmosphere that I have so carefully built up?

The poet seeks to express the quintessence of the whole experience and, consequently, each line and each thought-paragraph is wrought at a higher pitch of emotion than is the case in prose, and moreover, the use of rhythm demands a method of description or narration that achieves its effects more vividly and instantaneously than in prose writing. It will be felt incongruous if the more leisurely and less intense methods of prose are employed in a metrical composition. The very fact of writing poetry imposes on the poet an obligation to find a compressed and tense mode of speech which appeals shortly and vividly to the reader's emotions. Especially is this true of lyric poetry where every line must count and not a word be used which is not powerfully 'alive'.

How conscious poets are of this obligation to choose the right words may best be illustrated by giving some examples of revisions made in famous poems. Here first, is Keats' description of the fallen Saturn at the beginning of *Hyperion*.

> Upon the sodden ground
> His old right arm lay nerveless, listless, dead,
> Unsceptred; and his realmless eyes were closed;
> While his bow'd head seemed list'ning to the Earth,
> His ancient mother, for some comfort yet.

Originally Keats wrote, 'His old right hand lay nerveless on the ground' instead of the line as we now have it. Again, from the same poet we take the third stanza of the 'Ode to A Nightingale'.

> Fade far away, dissolve, and quite forget
>   What thou among the leaves hast never known,
> The weariness, the fever, and the fret
>   Here, where men sit and hear each other groan;
> Where palsy shakes a few, sad, last gray hairs,
>   Where youth grows pale, and spectre thin, and dies;
> Where but to think is to be full of sorrow
>   And leaden-eyed despairs,
> Where Beauty cannot keep her lustrous eyes,
>   Or new Love pine at them beyond tomorrow.

Line six at first read, 'Where youth grows pale and thin and old and dies.' Try to discover for yourself the reason for these changes. Ask these questions.

1 What change in meaning does the alteration make?
2 In what way is the second version more fitting for its context?
3 Is greater intensity achieved by the alteration, and if so, how?
4 Does the revised line give more aesthetic pleasure than the original, and if so, in what way?

The diction of poetry, like every other aspect of style, must constantly be judged according to its fitness for the task that the poet has set himself. From time to time in the history of criticism controversy has raged as to whether there are words which are too undignified to be used in poetry. Several times in the development of English Literature, movements of revolt have been started against the poetry of the preceding age which, it has been claimed, has been stilted and artificial, and altogether remote from 'deeds and language such as men do use'. Too often in these critical battles, it has been forgotten that the poet and his diction can only be judged rightly against the background of their purpose. The Elizabethans were followed by the Metaphysical Poets; these gave place to the Augustans; they, in their turn, were followed by the Romantics, against whom and their heirs–the Victorians and Georgians–the Modern Poets were in conscious revolt. These great swings of the pendulum mark the living rhythm of vitality and development : a static literature is a dead one, and ceaseless experiment is a condition of continuing life. Do not, then, join the school of criticism which pastes a label on a poet and imagines that it has, thereby, judged him. Any competent student can classify, by diction alone the following passages as 'Elizabethan', 'Metaphysical', 'Eighteenth Century', 'Romantic', and 'Modern' ; nobody can truly judge their poetic worth who does not seek to discover the poet's purpose, and then assess the value of his words in the light of that.

[A]

> My lady's presence makes the roses red,
> Because to see her lips they blush for shame ;
> The lilies' leaves, for envy, pale became,
> And her white hands in them this envy bred.
> The marigold her leaves abroad doth spread,
> Because the sun's and her power is the same ;
> The violet of purple colour came,
> Dyed in the blood she made my heart to shed.
> In brief, all flowers from her their virtue take :
> From her sweet breath their sweet smells do proceed,
> The living heat which her eye-beams doth make,
> Warmeth the ground, and quickeneth the seed.
> > The rain wherewith she watereth the flowers
> > Falls from mine eyes, which she dissolves in showers.

[B]

> Our two soules therefore, which are one,
> > Though I must goe, endure not yet
> A breach but an expansion,
> > Like gold to airy thinnesse beate.
>
> If they be two, they are two so
> > As stiffe twin compasses are two,
> Thy soule the fixt foote, makes no show
> > To move, but doth, if th' other doe.
>
> And though it in the center sit,
> > Yet when the other far doth rome,
> It leanes and hearkens after it,
> > And growes erect, as that comes home.

[C]

> Lo! where the rosy bosom'd Hours,
> Fair Venus' train appear,
> Disclose the long-expecting flowers,
> And wake the purple year!
> The Attic warbler pours her throat,
> Responsive to the cuckoo's note,
> The untaught harmony of spring:
> While, whisp'ring pleasure as they fly,
> Cool Zephyrs thro' the clear blue sky
> Their gathered fragrance fling.

[D]

> Are not the mountains, waves, and skies, a part
> Of me and of my soul, as I of them?
> Is not the love of these deep in my heart
> With a pure passion? should I not contemn
> All objects, if compared with these? and stem
> A tide of suffering, rather than forego
> Such feelings for the hard and worldly phlegm
> Of those whose eyes are only turn'd below,
> Gazing upon the ground, with thoughts which dare not glow?

[E]

> His soul stretched tight across the skies
> That fade behind a city block,
> Or trampled by insistent feet
> At four and five and six o'clock!
> And short square fingers stuffing pipes,
> And evening newspapers and eyes
> Assured of certain certainties,
> The conscience of a blackened street
> Impatient to assume the world.

In selecting the words which he will use, a poet is concerned with their meaning, their sound, and their associations. The sound of words will be dealt with in the next chapter; here we will consider meaning and associations. When Shakespeare wished to convey a sense of the rich profusion and daring of the Spring, he coined the phrase, 'proud-pied April'. Here, the meaning of the compound epithet is exact, but more important, its associations awake in the imaginative reader a picture of the young year throwing off the tyranny of Winter and standing out bravely in all its youthful and contrasting loveliness. Again, in *Antony and Cleopatra*, Antony expresses his sense of imminent defeat in these words.

> The hearts
> That spaniel'd me at heels, to whom I gave
> Their wishes, do discandy, melt their sweets
> On blossoming Caesar! and this pine is bark'd
> That overtopp'd them all.

Examine very carefully all the underlined words and consider them from the point of view of (*a*) meaning, and (*b*) associations. You will find that the richness of the words, the imagination-stirring quality that we call their 'poetry', comes primarily from the associations that they carry with them, and for which the poet has chosen them.

Adjectives and verbs are the chief sources of this richness of language which makes poetry appeal so strongly to the imagination, and in judging the artistic merit of the diction of a poem, the critic should look carefully at every adjective and verb employed. Here are a few general observations to help you in this part of the critic's task.

1 The greatest poetry obtains its effect by appealing to the imagination. Consequently, a bold sweep of the artist's brush is to be preferred to a meticulous etching in of details. Remember these words of Longinus: 'Precision in every detail comes perilously near littleness.' Here, for example, are two descriptions of country scenes.

[A]

> Screen'd is this nook o'er the high, half-reaped field,
>   And here till sun-down, shepherd! will I be.
> Through the thick corn the scarlet poppies peep,
>   And round green roots and yellowing stalks I see
> Pale pink convolvulus in tendrils creep.

83

[B]

> There sometimes does a leaping Fish
> Send through the Tarn a lonely chear;
> The crags repeat the Raven's croak,
> In symphony austere!
> Thither the Rainbow comes, the Cloud;
> And Mists that spread the flying shroud!
> And sun-beams! and the sounding blast,
> That, if it could, would hurry past,
> But that enormous Barrier binds it fast.

You will see at once that the second passage is the more imaginative of the two. The first is too much of an exact catalogue; the imagination does not respond to a page from a botanist's note-book. In the second, the appeal is entirely to the imagination, the reader is expected to respond actively. Note the sparing but evocative use of adjectives.

2 A successful use of diction appeals *swiftly* and *commandingly* to the imagination; in a flash we begin to see the pictures, and think the thoughts that the poet intended. Any suggestion of labour, of striving for effect, on the part of the poet is fatal, such poetry 'smells of the lamp'. Remember in this connexion what Keats said of poetry in general: 'If Poetry comes not as naturally as the leaves to a tree, it had better not come at all.' We do not at first extract the full richness from each word or phrase, but we are at once arrested by it, and made immediately aware of the magic that it holds. Consider these examples:

> Now silken dalliance in the wardrobe lies.

> . . . his virtues
> Will plead like angels, trumpet-tongued against
> The deep damnation of his taking off.

> . . . and thrush
> Through the echoing timber does so rinse and wring
> The ear, it strikes like lightning to hear him sing.

3 While the simple word is often the best, the obvious word is
  unpoetical. The poet's task is to reveal life at its most intense;
  to do this he must seize on the essence of a thing, his eye must
  catch the significant detail, and reveal it by the significant
  word. He perceives what ordinary men do not perceive,
  yet so words the matter that it comes to them as 'a rewording
  of their own best thoughts'. Compare these examples of
  the simple and the obvious:

[A]
> The golden sun in the blue sky.

[B]
> Golden lads and girls all must
> As chimney-sweepers come to dust.

[C]
> And on the far-flung hills, a purple heat-haze.

[D]
> Once more the Heavenly Power
> Makes all things new,
> And domes the red-plow'd hills
> With loving blue.

  When Shelley said that poets were the 'authors of language'
what he had in mind was not so much word-coining as the
use of familiar words in an entirely new way:

> . . . And so each venture
> Is a new beginning, a raid on the inarticulate . . .

PRACTICAL WORK

1

Discuss the descriptive words in the following passages, and
suggest alternatives where this is possible without damaging
the force of the original.

[A]

Steady fell the rain throughout the night
And cooled earth's fevered brow with welcome dew.
The thirsty fields imbibed the healthy mist,
That broke a month-long parching from the sun,
Whose golden beams were stifled the next morn
By heavy, black, and thick-encircling clouds.

[B]

But let the months go round, a few short months,
And all shall be restored. These naked shoots,
Barren as lances, among which the wind
Makes wintry music, sighing as it goes,
Shall put their graceful foliage on again,
And more aspiring, and with ampler spread,
Shall boast new charms, and more than they have lost.

[C]

Yet midst the Blaze of Courts she fixed her Love,
On the cool Fountain or the shady Grove;
Still with the Shepherd's Innocence her Mind
To the sweet Vale, and flow'ry Mead inclined.
And oft as Spring renewed the Plains with Flowers,
Breathed his soft Gales, and led the fragrant Hours,
With sure Return she sought the sylvan Scene,
The breezy Mountains, and the Forests green.

[D]

St Agnes' Eve – Ah, bitter chill it was!
The owl, for all his feathers, was a-cold;
The hare limp'd trembling through the frozen grass,
And silent were the flock in woolly fold:
Numb were the Beadsman's fingers while he told
His rosary, and while his frosted breath,
Like pious incense from a censer old,
Seem'd taking flight for Heaven, without a death,
Past the sweet Virgin's picture, while his prayer he saith.

[E]

With blackest moss the flower-plots
Were thickly crusted, one and all:

> The rusted nails fell from the knots
> > That held the peach to the garden-wall.
> The broken sheds look'd sad and strange:
> > Unlifted was the clinking latch!
> > Weeded and worn the ancient thatch
> Upon the lonely moated grange.

[F]

> . . . Thou wind, that ravest without,
> > Bare crag, or mountain-tarn, or blasted tree,
> Or pine-grove whither woodman never clomb,
> Or lonely house, long held the witches' home,
> > Methinks were fitter instruments for thee,
> Mad Lutanist! who in this month of showers,
> Of dark brown gardens, and of peeping flowers,
> Makest Devil's yule, with worse than wintry song,
> The blossoms, buds, and timorous leaves among.

2

Show clearly how the underlined words and phrases in the following appeal to the imagination by stirring up associations in the mind of the reader.

[A]

> A voice so thrilling ne'er was heard
> In spring-time from the cuckoo-bird,
> Breaking the silence of the seas
> Among the farthest Hebrides.

> Will no one tell me what she sings?
> Perhaps the plaintive numbers flow
> For old, unhappy, far-off things
> And battles long ago.

[B]

> That time of year thou may'st in me behold
> When yellow leaves, or none, or few, do hang
> Upon those boughs which shake against the cold,
> Bare ruined choirs where late the sweet birds sang.

87

[C]

> And how beguile you? Death has no repose
>   Warmer or deeper than that Orient sand
> Which hides the beauty and bright faith of those
>   Who made the Golden Journey to Samarkand.

[D]

> . . . he stood, and called
> His legions, Angel forms, who lay entranced,
> Thick as autumnal leaves that strow the brooks
> In Vallombrosa, where the Etrurian shades
> High over-arched embower.

3

What is the poet's intention in each of the following passages, and to what extent does his choice of words help or hinder him in his task?

[A]

> Heap cassia, sandal-buds and stripes
>   Of labdanum, and aloe-balls,
> Smeared with dull nard an Indian wipes
>   From out her hair: such balsam falls
>   Down sea-side mountain pedestals,
> From tree-tops where tired winds are fain,
> Spent with the vast and howling main
> To treasure half their Island-gain.
>
> And strew faint sweetness from some old
>   Egyptian's fine worm-eaten shroud
> Which breaks to dust when once unrolled;
>   Or shredded perfume, like a cloud
>   From closet long to quiet vowed,
>   With mothed and dropping arras hung,
>   Mouldering her lute and books among,
>   As when a queen, long dead, was young.

[B]

> 'What's that so black agin the sun?' said Files-on-Parade.
> 'It's Danny fightin' 'ard for life,' the Colour-Sergeant said.

'What's that that whimpers over'ead?' said Files-on-Parade.
'It's Danny's soul that's passin' now,' the Colour-Sergeant said.
   For they're done with Danny Deever, you can 'ear the
      quickstep play,
   The regiment's in column, an' they're marchin' us away;
   Ho! the young recruits are shakin', and they'll want their
      beer to-day,
   After hangin' Danny Deever in the mornin'!

[C]

And may at last my weary age
Find out the peaceful hermitage,
The hairy gown and mossy cell,
Where I may sit and rightly spell
Of every star that heaven doth shew
And every herb that sips the dew;
Till old experience do attain
To something like prophetic strain.
   These pleasures, Melancholy, give,
   And I with thee will choose to live.

[D]

Yet let me flap this bug with gilded wings,
This painted child of dirt, that stinks and stings;
Whose buzz the witty and the fair annoys,
Yet wit ne'er tastes, and beauty ne'er enjoys:
So well-bred spaniels civilly delight
In mumbling of the game they dare not bite.
Eternal smiles his emptiness betray,
As shallow streams run dimpling all the way.
Whether in florid impotence he speaks,
And, as the prompter breathes, the puppet squeaks;
Or at the ear of Eve, familiar toad!
Half froth, half venom, spits himself abroad,
In puns, or politics, or tales, or lies,
Or spite, or smut, or rhymes, or blasphemies.
His wit all see-saw, between that and this,
Now high, now low, now master up, now miss,
And he himself one vile antithesis.
Amphibious thing! that acting either part,

The trifling head, or the corrupted heart;
Fop at the toilet, flatterer at the board,
Now trips a lady, and now struts a lord.
Eve's tempter thus the Rabbins have express'd,
A cherub's face, a reptile all the rest.
Beauty that mocks you, parts that none will trust,
Wit that can creep, and pride that licks the dust.

[E]

Good sometimes queen, prepare thee hence for France.
Think I am dead, and that even here thou takest
As from my death-bed thy last living leave;
In winter's tedious nights sit by the fire
With good old folks, and let them tell thee tales
Of woeful ages long ago betid;   .
And e'er thou bid good night, to quit their griefs,
Tell thou the lamentable fall of me,
And send the hearers weeping to their beds;
For why, the senseless brands will sympathize
The heavy accent of thy moving tongue,
And in compassion weep the fire out,
And some will mourn in ashes, some coal-black,
For the deposing of a rightful king.

[F]

Strange fits of passion I have known:
And I will dare to tell,
But in the Lover's ear alone,
What once to me befell.

When she I lov'd was strong and gay,
And like a rose in June,
I to her cottage bent my way,
Beneath an evening Moon.

Upon the Moon I fix'd my eye,
All over the wide lea:
My horse trudged on—and we drew nigh
Those paths so dear to me.

And now we reach'd the orchard plot:
And, as we climb'd the hill,
Towards the roof of Lucy's cot
The moon descended still.

In one of those sweet dreams I slept,
Kind Nature's gentlest boon!
And, all the while, my eyes I kept
On the descending Moon.

My Horse mov'd on; hoof after hoof
He rais'd, and never stopp'd:
When down behind the cottage roof,
At once, the planet dropp'd.

What fond and wayward thoughts will slide
Into a Lover's head—
'O mercy!' to myself I cried,
'If Lucy should be dead!'

[G]

A slumber did my spirit seal,
   I had no human fears:
She seem'd a thing that could not feel
   The touch of earthly years.

No motion has she now, no force;
   She neither hears nor sees;
Roll'd round in earth's diurnal course,
   With rocks, and stones, and trees!

[H]

Tiger, tiger, burning bright
In the forests of the night,
What immortal hand or eye
Could frame thy fearful symmetry?

In what distant deeps or skies
Burnt the fire of thine eyes?
On what wings dare he aspire?
What the hand dare seize the fire?

> And what shoulder and what art
> Could twist the sinews of thy heart?
> And, when thy heart began to beat,
> What dread hand? and what dread feet?
>
> What the hammer? What the chain?
> In what furnace was thy brain?
> What the anvil? What dread grasp
> Dare its deadly terrors clasp?
>
> When the stars threw down their spears,
> And watered heaven with their tears,
> Did he smile his work to see?
> Did he who made the lamb make thee?
>
> Tiger, tiger, burning bright
> In the forests of the night,
> What immortal hand or eye
> Dare frame thy fearful symmetry?

[I]

> When reddening dawn rose o'er the darkling plain,
> Her quickening beams the shadows soon 'gan wane;
> But swift from out the ground sprang gloomy Dis
> And fronted Phoebus' face with sullen phiz.

4

In each of the following passages you will find examples of word-coining, of compound adjectives, or the use of proper nouns. Discuss their purpose and their effectiveness.

[A]

> Now crouch, ye kings of greatest Asia,
> And tremble, when ye hear this scourge will come
> That whips down cities and controlleth crowns,
> Adding their wealth and treasure to my store.
> The Euxine sea, north to Natolia;
> The Terrene, west; the Caspian, north north-east;
> And on the south, Sinus Arabicus;
> Shall all be loaden with the martial spoils
> We will convey with us to Persia.

Then shall my native city Samarcanda,
And crystal waves of fresh Jaertis' stream,
The pride and beauty of her princely seat,
Be famous through the furthest continents;
For there my palace royal shall be plac'd,
Whose shining turrets shall dismay the heavens,
And cast the fame of Ilion's tower to hell:
Through the streets, with troops of conquered kings,
I'll ride in golden armour like the sun.

[B]

And still she slept an azure-lidded sleep,
In blanched linen, smooth and lavender'd,
While he from forth the closet brought a heap
Of candied apple, quince, and plum, and gourd;
With jellies soother than the creamy curd,
And lucent syrups, tinct with cinnamon;
Manna and dates, in argosy transferred
From Fez; and spiced dainties, every one,
From silken Samarcand to cedar'd Lebanon.

[C]

Glory be to God for dappled things—
    For skies of couple-colour as a brinded cow;
        For rose-moles all in stipple upon trout that swim;
Fresh-firecoal chestnut-falls; finches' wings;
Landscape plotted and pieced—fold, fallow, and plough;
        And all trádes, their gear and tackle and trim.

All things counter, original, spare, strange;
    Whatever is fickle, freckled (who knows how?)
        With swift, slow; sweet, sour; adazzle, dim;
He fathers-forth whose beauty is past change:
        Praise him.

[D]

This wimpled, whining, purblind, wayward boy
This senior-junior, giant-dwarf, Dan Cupid;
Regent of love-rhymes, lord of folded arms,
The anointed sovereign of sighs and groans,
Liege of all loiterers and malcontents.

5

Here are some examples of description by suggestion and description by enumeration of detail. Examine them carefully, and discuss the respective merits of the two methods in relation to the task attempted in each case.

[A]

> He scarce had ceased when the superior Fiend
> Was moving toward the shore; his ponderous shield,
> Ethereal temper, massy, large, and round,
> Behind him cast. The broad circumference
> Hung on his shoulders like the moon, whose orb
> Through optic glass the Tuscan artist views
> At evening from the top of Fesolè,
> Or in Valdarno, to descry new lands,
> Rivers, or mountains, in her spotty globe.
> His spear—to equal which the tallest pine
> Hewn on Norwegian hills to be the mast
> Of some great ammiral, were but a wand—
> He walked with.

[B]

> His visage seem'd
> In length and bulk, as doth the pine that tops
> Saint Peter's Roman fane, and the other bones
> Of like proportion, so that from above
> The bank, which girdled him below, such height
> Arose his stature, that three Friezelanders
> Had striven in vain to reach but to his hair,
> Full thirty ample palms was he exposed
> Downward from whence a man his garment loops.

[C]

> She was a Goddess of the infant world;
> By her in stature the tall Amazon
> Had stood a pigmy's height: she would have ta'en
> Achilles by the hair and bent his neck;
> Or with a finger stay'd Ixion's wheel.
> Her face was large as that of Memphian sphinx,
> Pedestal'd haply in a palace court,
> When sages look'd to Egypt for their lore.

[D]

Fresh carved cedar, mimicking a glade
Of palm and plantain, met from either side,
High in the midst in honour of the bride:
Two palms and then two plantains, and so on,
From either side their stems branch'd one to one
All down the aisled place; and beneath all
There ran a stream of lamps straight on from wall to wall.
So canopied, lay an untasted feast
Teeming with odours. Lamia, regal drest,
Silently paced about, and as she went,
In pale contented sort of discontent,
Mission'd her viewless servants to enrich
The fretted splendour of each nook and niche.
Between the tree-stems, marbled plain at first,
Came jasper panels; then, anon, there burst
Forth creeping imagery of slighter trees,
And with the larger wove small intricacies.

.   .   .   .

Of wealthy lustre was the banquet-room,
Fill'd with pervading brilliance and perfume:
Before each lucid panel fuming stood
A censer fed with myrrh and spiced wood,
Each by a sacred tripod held aloft,
Whose slender feet wide-swerv'd upon the soft
Wool-woofed carpets: fifty wreaths of smoke
From fifty censers their light voyage took
To the high roof, still mimick'd as they rose
Along the mirror'd walls by twin-clouds odorous.
Twelve sphered tables, by silk seats insphered,
High as the level of a man's breast rear'd
On libbard's paws, upheld the heavy gold
Of cups and goblets, and the store thrice told
Of Ceres' horn, and, in huge vessels, wine
Came from the gloomy tun with merry shine.
Thus loaded with a feast the tables stood,
Each shrining in the midst the image of a God.

[E]

Anon from out the earth, a fabric huge
Rose like an exhalation, with the sound
Of dulcet symphonies and voices sweet,
Built like a temple, where pilasters round
Were set, and Doric pillars overlaid
With golden architrave; nor did there want
Cornice of frieze, with bossy sculptures graven;
The roof was fretted gold. Not Babylon,
Nor great Alcairo, such magnificence
Equalled in all their glories, to enshrine
Belus or Serapis their gods, or seat
Their kings, when Egypt with Assyria strove
In wealth and luxury. The ascending pile
Stood fixed her stately highth, and straight the doors,
Opening their brazen folds, discover, wide
Within, her ample spaces o'er the smooth
And level pavement: from the arched roof,
Pendent by subtle magic, many a row
Of starry lamps and blazing cressets, fed
With naphtha and asphaltus, yielded light
As from a sky.

5
Style: Imagery and figures of speech

Imagery in poetry is an appeal to the senses through words. Through the senses the emotions and intellect of the reader can be swiftly stirred; consequently, poetry makes much use of imagery. This is not to say that all good poetry must contain imagery; take, for example, this poem by John Donne, which is almost bare of imagery in the normal sense of the word, but which, nevertheless, is emotionally and intellectually powerful, working through directly logical statements and a subtle use of vestigial images (*eg* 'will now extend His vast prerogative' which suggests movement and space; 'why murmure I' which suggests sound). But there is nothing here of the *directly* sensuous image that is so frequent elsewhere in poetry. In every individual poem with which he deals, the critic must decide the reason for, and weigh the effectiveness of, the use or disuse of such imagery.

LOVES DEITIE

I long to talk with some old lovers ghost,
　Who dyed before the god of Love was borne:
I cannot thinke that hee, who then lov'd most,
　Sunke so low, as to love one which did scorne.
But since this god produc'd a destinie,
And that vice-nature, custome, lets it be;
　I must love her, that loves not mee.

Sure, they which made him god, meant not so much,
　Nor he, in his young godhead practis'd it;
But when an even flame two hearts did touch,

His office was indulgently to fit
Actives to passives. Correspondencie
Only his subject was; It cannot bee
   Love, till I love her, that loves mee.

But every moderne god will now extend
   His vast prerogative, as far as Jove.
To rage, to lust, to write to, to commend,
   All is the purlewe of the God of Love.
Oh were wee wak'ned by this Tyrannie
To ungod this child againe, it could not bee
   I should love her, who loves not mee.

Rebell and Atheist too, why murmure I, .
   As though I felt the worst that love could doe?
Love might make me leave loving, or might trie
   A deeper plague, to make her love me too,
Which, since she loves before, I'm loth to see;
Falshood is worse than hate; and that must bee,
   If shee whom I love, should love mee.

We must be clear first of all, that imagery, diction, and versification alike, are an expression of the way in which a poet conceives his theme. In this book, we devote separate chapters to each of these aspects of style in order to deal with each in greater detail. In criticising a poem, however, we avoid such an abstraction, and try to see each as a part of the poet's expression of his theme, and to observe the inter-relationship of each with the others. In the criticism in Chapter 7 you will notice that section D treats the style of the poem in this manner. See, too, pp. 111–114 of this chapter.

Images can be classified according to the sense to which they are directed: sound; sight (colour or shape images); taste; smell; touch (thermal or tactile images); movement (kinaes-thetic images). Rupert Brooke's famous poem, 'The Old Vicarage, Grantchester', provides examples of each of these.

Ah God! to see the branches stir   } *kinaesthetic*
Across the moon at Grantchester!   }
To smell the thrilling–sweet and rotten, } *smell*
Unforgettable, unforgotten   }
River-smell, and hear the breeze } *sound*
Sobbing in the little trees.   }
Say, do the elm-clumps greatly stand, }
Still guardians of that holy land?   }   *shape–suggested*
The chestnuts shade, in reverend dream,
The yet unacademic stream?
Is dawn a secret shy and cold } *colour and thermal*
Anadyomene, silver-gold?   }
And sunset still a golden sea
From Haslingfield to Madingley?
And after, ere the night is born,
Do hares come out about the corn?
Oh, is the water sweet and cool,
Gentle and brown, above the pool?
And laughs the immortal river still
Under the mill, under the mill?
Say,.is there Beauty yet to find?
And Certainty? and Quiet kind?
Deep meadows yet, for to forget
The lies, and truths, and pain? . . . oh! yet
Stands the Church clock at ten to three? }
And is there honey still for tea?   } *taste–suggested*

In judging a poem we should notice carefully the kind of
images used, and any alterations in the image-patterns or
emphasis which may be seen as the theme develops. For
example, in this poem by Charles Kingsley, colour and
kinaesthetic images are used to point the contrast between
verses one and two, and so sustain the theme. The dominant
colour in verse one is green, in verse two it is brown. The
kinaesthetic images in the first verse are brisk and lively, in the
second they drag.

YOUNG AND OLD

When all the world is young, lad,
  And all the trees are green;
And every goose a swan, lad,
  And every lass a queen;
Then hey for boot and horse, lad,
  And round the world away;
Young blood must have its course, lad,
  And every dog his day.

When all the world is old, lad,
  And all the trees are brown;
And all the sport is stale, lad,
  And all the wheels run down;
Creep home, and take your place there,
  The spent and maimed among;
God grant you find one face there,
  You loved when all was young.

In Hardy's poem 'In The Small Hours' there is a remarkable use of kinaesthetic imagery which sustains the theme most vividly. The light movement of the first two verses is prolonged into the third verse, when suddenly the line, 'Had longwhiles stilled amain', brings the dream revelry to an end, and, with no change in rhythm, the movement of the poem yet slows to a crawl which matches the reluctance of the dreamer to admit 'That Now, not Then, held reign'.

I lay in my bed and fiddled
  With a dreamland viol and bow
And the tunes flew back to my fingers
  I had melodied years ago.
It was two or three in the morning
  When I fancy-fiddled so
Long reels and country-dances,
  And hornpipes swift and slow.

And soon anon came crossing
  The chamber in the gray

Figures of jigging fieldfolk –
　　Saviours of corn and hay –
To the air of 'Haste to the Wedding,'
　　As after a wedding-day;
Yea, up and down the middle
　　In windless whirls went they!

There danced the bride and bridegroom,
　　And couples in a train,
Gay partners time and travail
　　Had longwhiles stilled amain! . . .
It seemed a thing for weeping
　　To find, at slumber's wane
And morning's sly increeping,
　　That Now, not Then, held reign.

In Keats' 'Ode to Autumn' the rich profusion of the imagery has blinded many readers to the careful pattern which it follows. The images in verse one describe the fruits and flowers of autumn; in verse two, the occupations of autumn are the theme; verse three is full of autumnal sounds. Underlying this image-pattern, there is a time movement also conveyed by the imagery. Verse one with its mists is morning; verse two is hushed with the heat of noon and early afternoon; verse three has moved on to evening with the sound of gnats, lambs, and crickets, and gathering swallows to provide 'music at·the close'. Thus the imagery sustains the poet's purpose which was to give in his comparatively short poem, the quintessence of the season.

Season of mists and mellow fruitfulness,
　　Close bosom-friend of the maturing sun;
Conspiring with him how to load and bless
　　With fruit the vines that round the thatch-eaves run;
To bend with apples the moss'd cottage-trees,
　　And fill all fruit with ripeness to the core;
　　　To swell the gourd, and plump the hazel shells
　　With a sweet kernel; to set budding more,
And still more, later flowers for the bees,

Until they think warm days will never cease,
    For Summer has o'er-brimm'd their clammy cells.

Who hath not seen thee oft amid thy store?
    Sometimes whoever seeks abroad may find
Thee sitting careless on a granary floor,
    Thy hair soft-lifted by the winnowing wind;
Or on a half-reap'd furrow sound asleep,
    Drows'd with the fume of poppies, while thy hook
        Spares the next swath and all its twined flowers:
And sometimes like a gleaner thou dost keep
    Steady thy laden head across a brook;
    Or by a cyder-press, with patient look,
        Thou watchest the last oozings hours by hours.

Where are the songs of Spring? Ay, where are they?
    Think not of them, thou hast thy music too,–
While barrèd clouds bloom the soft-dying day;
    And touch the stubble-plains with rosy hue;
Then in a wailful choir the small gnats mourn
    Among the river sallows, borne aloft
        Or sinking as the light wind lives or dies;
And full-grown lambs loud bleat from hilly bourn;
    Hedge-crickets sing; and now with treble soft
    The red-breast whistles from a garden-croft;
        And gathering swallows twitter in the skies.

Most poets have their favourite images or image-groups: certain sense impressions haunt them throughout life, or throughout particular periods of their lives. Caroline Spurgeon's book, *Shakespeare's Imagery*, showed that each of the tragedies has a dominant image-motif, a significant key-note enabling us to grasp the theme of each play with greater certainty. *Hamlet* is dominated by sickness and disease images; blood and darkness are prominent in *Macbeth*; *Othello* contains a great number of animal images; *Lear* is full of images of suffering and torture. Miss Spurgeon's researches confirmed too what had often been guessed, that in Shakespeare's plays as a whole, nature images easily occupy the first place. Compare this with Milton's poetry in which images drawn from books predominate over those drawn from nature. In *Paradise Lost* (*Books I and II*) for example, images drawn from the Classics, the Bible, or legendary sources occupy first place; images drawn from the forces of nature (*eg* thunder) come second; images based on the life of mankind on earth are third in quantity; and images drawn from natural objects are fourth. Matthew Arnold's poetry is full of moon images which symbolise the

> Plainness and clearness without shadow of stain
> Clearness divine!

– the ideal towards which he so steadfastly struggled. Middleton Murry noted how in *Hyperion* (*Book III*) Keats suddenly suffuses the poem with his favourite colour, red, marking as it were, a dramatic break in style and emotion in a poem whose dominant colours up to that point have been green, grey, silver and black. The deification of Apollo is heralded by a riot of crimson and red.

> Flush everything that hath a vermeil hue,
> Let the rose grow intense and warm the air,
> And let the clouds of even and of morn
> Float in voluptuous fleeces o'er the hills;
> Let the red wine within the goblet boil,
> Cold as a bubbling well; let faint-lipp'd shells,
> On sands, or in great deeps, vermilion turn
> Through all their labyrinths.

Those examples will serve to stress the general importance of a careful study of imagery. We must return now to particular cases.

Imagery is used to move emotion. To do this, it employs two different methods; description and symbolising. Of course, many images make use of both methods, but such a distinction can be made and is useful when we are trying to deepen our understanding of imagery. It is essential to understand exactly what a poet means by the images he is using, and to decide whether they are descriptive or symbolic, or both, since we cannot otherwise be sure that the full imaginative sympathy which should exist between poet and critic has been established.

Descriptive imagery works both by simple representation of the thing described and by suggestion. Take these lines by Arnold (from *Sohrab and Rustum*):

> As some rich woman, on a winter's morn,
> Eyes through her silken curtains the poor drudge
> Who with numb blacken'd fingers makes her fire –
> At cock-crow, on a starlit winter's morn,
> When the frost flowers the whiten'd window-panes –
> And wonders how she lives, and what the thoughts
> Of that poor drudge may be; so Rustum eyed
> The unknown adventurous youth, who from afar
> Came seeking Rustum, and defying forth
> All the most valiant chiefs.

Each image used here is purely descriptive and rather poor in associative power. There is no depth in the picture – it is on the surface, one-dimensional. More truly poetical, because more suggestive, is Keat's description of the fallen Titans in *Hyperion* (*Book II*).

> But for the main, here found they covert drear.
> Scarce images of life, one here, one there,
> Lay vast and edgeways, like a dismal cirque
> Of Druid stones, upon a forlorn moor,
> When the chill rain begins at shut of eve,
> In dull November, and their chancel vault,
> The Heaven itself, is blinded throughout night.
> Each one kept shroud, nor to his neighbour gave
> Or word, or look, or action of despair.

Notice how much richer in 'background' the images are here. The reader's imagination is stimulated to gather together all

the associations that such words as 'dismal cirque of Druid stones', 'forlorn moor', 'chill rain', 'shut of eve', 'dull November', 'chancel vault', have for it. Let us try to analyse the richness of one of these phrases. We can express our reactions to it most simply in diagrammatic form.

In the diagram above the inmost circle represents our *immediate* reactions to the words; the next, those suggested by the first reactions; and so on. All the associations that each word carries are inter-related, so that the full image, though the sum of its parts, is yet infinitely richer than a mere total could be, since the parts are *emotionally* fused to form the whole. Examine the other images in the passage with equal care, and you will find that the same is true of each; you will notice, too, the interlocking of the separate images. For example, the religious associations of 'Druid' are caught up again (with a difference) in 'chancel vault'; and 'dismal cirque' and 'forlorn moor' are in emotional harmony.

One of the weaknesses of the simile that we quoted from *Sohrab and Rustum* was its over-elaboration. Poetry should be 'simple, sensuous and passionate', said Milton, and though we must be careful about the meaning we attach to the first word of his description, we can be quite clear that he meant that it should be *immediate* in its appeal, even though it will not perhaps yield its full riches without long siege. Arnold can achieve a masterly economy in his imagery at times, as this extract will show. He is describing the river of Time as it bears man to the solemn fulfilment of life.

> And the width of the waters, the hush
> Of the grey expanse where he floats,
> Freshening its current and spotted with foam
> As it draws to the Ocean, may strike
> Peace to the soul of the man on its breast—
> As the pale waste widens around him,
> As the banks fade dimmer away,
> As the stars come out, and the night-wind
> Brings up the stream
> Murmurs and scents of the infinite sea.

The images here are immediate in their effect and highly imaginative in the way in which each sound, shape, or colour appeal is backed by an emotional association which sustains and enriches the theme.

Concreteness and economy are the distinguishing marks of good imagery. Describing the mute sufferings of unrequited love, Viola in *Twelfth Night* uses the vivid image:

> She sat like patience on a monument,
> Smiling at grief.

How exact the description is, and yet how suggestive. The dull stupor into which misery has plunged her is startlingly conveyed by the macabre reference to 'monumental mockery'. Notice particularly here the mingling of the abstract and the concrete – 'sat like patience'; 'smiling at grief'. This device, so characteristic of Shakespeare, is extremely powerful because of its combination of sensuous with emotional and intellectual appeal. An effective image provides the reader's imagination with a stimulus in the shape of a vivid, concrete detail; the imagination is then called upon to do the rest through the associated ideas which the detail arouses.

Consideration of the examples that we have already given will by now have begun to make clear the functions of imagery. Used sometimes solely for its sensuous appeal, it is often used to stir up emotions and thoughts which lie behind the sense appeal; this is the symbolical use of imagery to which we referred earlier in this chapter. First, let us look at imagery used solely as a stimulus of the senses. Here is an early sonnet by Keats.

ON LEAVING SOME FRIENDS AT AN EARLY HOUR

Give me a golden pen, and let me lean
  On heap'd up flowers, in regions clear, and far;
  Bring me a tablet whiter than a star,
Or hand of hymning angel, when 'tis seen
The silver strings of heavenly harp atween:
  And let there glide by many a pearly car,
  Pink robes, and wavy hair, and diamond tiar,
And half-discovered wings, and glances keen.
The while let music wander round my ears,
  And as it reaches each delicious ending,
  Let me write down a line of glorious tone,
And full of many wonders of the spheres:
  For what a height my spirit is contending!
  'Tis not content so soon to be alone.

This is cloying, but Keats learnt to avoid decoration for decoration's sake. He came to realise that purely descriptive

imagery should flash its message instantaneously to the senses
as in his sonnet, 'Bright Star'.

> Bright star, would I were stedfast as thou art—
>   Not in lone splendour hung aloft the night
> And watching, with eternal lids apart,
>   Like nature's patient, sleepless Eremite,
> The moving waters at their priestlike task
>   Of pure ablution round earth's human shores,
> Or gazing on the new soft-fallen mask
>   Of snow upon the mountains and the moors—
> No—yet still stedfast, still unchangeable,
>   Pillow'd upon my fair love's ripening breast,
> To feel for ever its soft fall and swell,
>   Awake for ever in a sweet unrest,
> Still, still to hear her tender-taken breath,
> And so live ever—or else swoon to death.

The imagery here is wholly sensuous, but it is much more
powerful than that in the previous sonnet, for it gets its effect
not by the piling up of details, but by seizing upon the
significant ones.

Keats learnt too the use of symbolical imagery. In this
sonnet the imagery works by arousing thoughts and emotions
which are fused with the concreteness of the basic images.

THE HUMAN SEASONS

> Four seasons fill the measure of the year;
>   There are four seasons in the mind of man:
> He has his lusty Spring, when fancy clear
>   Takes in all Beauty with an easy span:
> He has his Summer, when luxuriously
>   Spring's honied cud of youthful thought he loves
> To ruminate, and by such dreaming nigh
>   His nearest unto Heaven: quiet coves
> His soul has in its Autumn, when his wings
>   He furleth close; contented so to look

> On mists in idleness – to let fair things
>   Pass by unheeded as a threshold brook.
> He has his Winter too of pale misfeature,
> Or else he would forego his mortal nature.

Analyse for yourself the relative value of the sensuous and emotional content of such images as,

> Spring's honied cud . . .

> . . . contented so to look
> On mists in idleness . . .

> He has his Winter too of pale misfeature . . .

The symbolic use of imagery reaches its zenith in metaphor, the most intense form that imagery can take. Metaphor identifies two distinct objects and fuses them unforgettably in a white heat of imagination. So swiftly does it work, that it often finds expression in one word, and the sense impression that it conveys is always subordinate to the emotional and intellectual associations that it is its business to arouse. In the following, for example, the appeal to our senses is only half-consciously realised, so swiftly is this succeeded by a powerful stirring of the emotions and intellect.

[A]
> Falstaff sweats to death
> And *lards* the lean earth as he walks along.

[B]
> Why what a *candy* deal of courtesy
> This fawning *greyhound* then did proffer me!

[C]
> To put down Richard, that sweet, lovely *rose*,
> And plant this *thorn*, this *canker*, Bollingbroke.

This symbolism is perhaps the most prominent feature of Shakespeare's mature and late styles. Our imagination is fired directly and powerfully by it, but an analysis of the connexion between stimulus and final impression would be long and difficult. Consider this example from *Antony and Cleopatra*. Cleopatra is lamenting Antony's death:

> Hast thou no care of me? shall I abide
> In this dull world; which in thy absence is
> No better than a sty? O! see my women,
> The crown o' the earth doth melt. My lord!
> O! withered is the garland of the war,
> The soldier's pole is fall'n; young boys and girls
> Are level now with men; the odds is gone,
> And there is nothing left remarkable
> Beneath the visiting moon.

The way in which metaphor is used is a major test of poetic ability; only the greatest can handle it greatly. It fuses dissimilar objects into a new unity, and

> By observation of affinities
> In objects where no brotherhood exists
> To common minds

creates in its imaginative truth 'a new heaven and a new earth', giving us glimpses of 'the light that never was on sea or land'. It should appear unforced and spontaneous. If too remote from common experience, it will merely shock, or provoke that damning comment, 'How clever!' If too close to common experience, it will be a cliché. Its function is to lead us from the known to the unknown; to enable us to look through the

> . . . magic casements, opening on the foam
> Of perilous seas, in faery lands forlorn.

Great metaphors, like poetry itself, should 'surprise by a fine excess', and yet have the unmistakable ring of imaginative truth.

It is time now to gather up the threads of our chapters on style before we turn, in the next chapter, to the way in which the critic's final judgement of a poem is formed. In so doing we shall learn to listen to the sound of the poet's words, and to realise how this harmonises with his imagery and his versification, to form a fit medium for the expression of his theme. Here, first of all, is 'Silver', by Walter de la Mare.

> Slowly, silently, now the moon
> Walks the night in her silver shoon;
> This way, and that, she peers, and sees
> Silver fruit upon silver trees;
> One by one the casements catch
> Her beams beneath the silvery thatch;
> Couched in his kennel, like a log,
> With paws of silver sleeps the dog;
> From their shadowy cote the white breasts peep
> Of doves in a silver-feathered sleep;
> A harvest mouse goes scampering by,
> With silver claws, and silver eye;
> And moveless fish in the water gleam,
> By silver reeds in a silver stream.

This is an impressionistic poem filled with the hush of the moonlit night that it describes. Each image is clear, and each is silvered, yet monotony is avoided partly by the frequent variation of rhyme, partly by the wonderful variety of image shapes which underlies the constant colour imagery. And the quiet, where does that come from? Notice the preponderance over all other sounds of the soft *s*; the avoidance of any harsh or strident vowel and consonant combinations; the slow, falling rhythm in duple time with occasional counterpointing to give the ear delight without, however, disturbing the quiet note of the basic rhythm. What movement there is belongs to the moon's stately wheeling through the still night, and the harvest mouse whose scampering contrasts with and emphasises the stillness of all life else, and yet, for all its motion, is

caught by the moon who lays her charm on claws and eye.
  Take for contrast these lines by Browning:

> I sprang to the stirrup, and Joris, and he;
> I galloped, Dirck galloped, we galloped all three,
> 'Good speed!' cried the watch, as the gate-bolts undrew;
> 'Speed!' echoed the wall to us galloping through;
> Behind shut the postern, the lights sank to rest,
> And into the midnight we galloped abreast.

The poet has chosen a theme of rapid action. Haste and urgency must fill every line of his poem. He expresses this theme, of course, in triple time with a rising rhythm so that the very sound of hoof-beats can be heard. But this is only a beginning. He concentrates on auditory and kinaesthetic imagery, for the eye has little time to notice details of colour and shape when the body is whirled into such frantic motion as this. Just a mention of the dwindling lights of the town, a hint of the blackness into which the men are riding – that is all. More vividly still, he contrives to keep the ear itself in a state of constant excitement. A sample line ten words long yields a count of ten different vowel sounds. A line from *Silver*, on the other hand, just two words shorter, has only five distinct vowel sounds; the ear is soothed and lulled.

$$\overset{1}{\text{'Good}} \ \overset{2}{\text{speed!'}} \ \overset{3}{\text{cried}} \ \overset{4}{\text{the}} \ \overset{5}{\text{watch}} \ \overset{6}{\text{as}} \ \overset{4}{\text{the}} \ \overset{7}{\text{gate}}\text{-}\overset{8}{\text{bolts}} \ \overset{9}{\text{un}}\overset{10}{\text{drew}}$$
$$\overset{1}{\text{This}} \ \overset{2}{\text{way,}} \ \overset{3}{\text{and}} \ \overset{3}{\text{that,}} \ \overset{4}{\text{she}} \ \overset{5}{\text{peers}} \ \overset{3}{\text{and}} \ \overset{4}{\text{sees}}$$

But then, you see, the two poets have two very different purposes which are reflected in every detail of their poems.
  These lines from Browning's *Soliloquy of the Spanish Cloister* again illustrate vividly how all the elements of style are welded to sustain and reinforce the theme:

> GR-R-R there go, my heart's abhorrence!
> Water your damned flower-pots, do!

> If hate killed men, Brother Lawrence,
>   God's blood, would not mine kill you!
> What? your myrtle-bush wants trimming?
>   Oh, that rose has prior claims—
> Needs its leaden vase filled brimming?
>   Hell dry you up with its flames!

Analyse their effect, noting particularly the repetition of 'r's and 'g's in the first few lines, and the way in which the poet achieves the sudden surge of intensified hatred in lines four and eight.

We have carefully avoided the use of the words 'alliteration' and 'onomatopoeia' in this discussion of the sound of poetry. They are useful terms and their meaning should be known, but too often they are used as convenient labels which, when affixed to a poem, spare the critic any further trouble. Close study of the sound of a poem *in relation to the poet's purpose as a whole* is what is needed, rather than a cursory identification of the figures of speech employed. Merely to call it alliterative will not take us very far towards a comprehension of the magic of this sonnet by Hopkins:

> As kingfishers catch fire, dragonflies dráw fláme;
> As tumbled over rim in roundy wells
> Stones ring; like each tucked string tells, each hung bell's
> Bow swung finds tongue to fling out broad its name;
> Each mortal thing does one thing and the same:
> Deals out that being indoors each one dwells;
> Selves—goes itself; *myself* it speaks and spells,
> Crying *Whát I dó is me: for that I came.*
> Í say móre: the just man justices;
> Kéeps gráce: thát keeps all his goings graces;
> Acts in God's eye what in God's eye he is—
> Chríst—for Christ plays in ten thousand places,
> Lovely in limbs, and lovely in eyes not his
> To the Father through the features of men's faces.

PRACTICAL WORK

In the following passages, show how figures of speech, imagery, and versification are used to sustain and reinforce the theme or to strengthen description. The analyses given on pages 111–114 form useful models. Pay careful attention to the *kind* of imagery used and its appropriateness to the work in hand; notice the use of image-patterns, and the interplay of sound and sense.

[A]

> Here with a Loaf of Bread beneath the Bough,
> A Flask of Wine, a Book of Verse—and Thou
>   Beside me singing in the Wilderness—
> And Wilderness is Paradise enow.
>
> 'How sweet is mortal Sovranty!'—think some:
> Others—'How blest the Paradise to come!'
>   Ah, take the Cash in hand and waive the Rest;
> Oh, the brave Music of a *distant* Drum!
>
> Look to the Rose that blows about us—'Lo,
> Laughing,' she says, 'into the World I blow:
>   At once the silken Tassel of my Purse
> Tear, and its Treasure on the Garden throw.'
>
> The Worldly Hope men set their Hearts upon
> Turns Ashes—or it prospers; and anon,
>   Like Snow upon the Desert's dusty Face
> Lighting a little Hour or two—is gone.
>
> And those who husbanded the Golden Grain,
> And those who flung it to the Winds like Rain,
>   Alike to no such aureate Earth are turn'd
> As, buried once, Men want dug up again.
>
> Think, in this battered Caravanserai
> Whose Doorways are alternate Night and Day,
>   How Sultan after Sultan with his Pomp
> Abode his Hour or two, and went his way.

They say the Lion and the Lizard keep
The Courts where Jamshyd gloried and drank deep;
    And Bahram, that great Hunter–the Wild Ass
Stamps o'er his Head, and he lies fast asleep.

I sometimes think that never blows so red
The Rose as where some buried Caesar bled;
    That every Hyacinth the Garden wears
Dropt in its Lap from some once lovely Head.

And this delightful Herb whose tender Green
Fledges the River's Lip on which we lean–
    Ah! lean upon it lightly! for who knows
From what once lovely Lip it springs unseen.

[B]

Break, break, break,
    On thy cold gray stones, O Sea!
And I would that my tongue could utter
    The thoughts that arise in me.

O well for the fisherman's boy,
    That he shouts with his sister at play!
O well for the sailor lad,
    That he sings in his boat on the bay!

And the stately ships go on
    To their haven under the hill;
But O for the touch of a vanished hand,
    And the sound of a voice that is still!

Break, break, break,
    At the foot of thy crags, O Sea!
But the tender grace of a day that is dead
    Will never come back to me.

[C]

Two Voices are there; one is of the Sea,
One of the Mountains; each a mighty Voice:
In both from age to age Thou didst rejoice,
They were thy chosen Music, Liberty!
There came a Tyrant, and with holy glee

Thou fought'st against Him; but hast vainly striven;
Thou from thy Alpine Holds at length art driven,
Where not a torrent murmurs heard by thee.
Of one deep bliss thine ear hath been bereft:
Then cleave, O cleave to that which still is left!
For, high-soul'd Maid, what sorrow would it be
That mountain Floods should thunder as before,
And Ocean bellow from his rocky shore,
And neither awful Voice be heard by thee!

[D]

So far, so fast the egyre drave,
The heart had hardly time to beat
Before a shallow, seething wave
Sobb'd in the grasses at our feet:
The feet had hardly time to flee
Before it brake against the knee
And all the world was in the sea.

[E]

Strew on her roses, roses,
   And never a spray of yew!
In quiet she reposes;
   Ah, would that I did too!

Her mirth the world required;
   She bathed it in smiles of glee.
But her heart was tired, tired,
   And now they let her be.

Her life was turning, turning,
   In mazes of heat and sound.
But for peace her soul was yearning,
   And now peace laps her round.

Her cabin'd, ample spirit,
   It flutter'd and fail'd for breath.
To-night it doth inherit
   The vasty hall of death.

[F]

SAMSON LAMENTS

O dark, dark, dark, amid the blaze of noon,
Irrecoverably dark, total eclipse
Without all hope of day!
O first-created beam, and thou great Word,
'Let there be light, and light was over all,'
Why am I thus bereaved thy prime decree?
The Sun to me is dark
And silent as the Moon
When she deserts the night,
Hid in her vacant interlunar cave.

[G]

The gray sea, and the long black land;
And the yellow half-moon large and low;
And the startled little waves that leap
In fiery ringlets from their sleep,
As I gain the cove with pushing prow,
And quench its speed i' the slushy sand.

Then a mile of warm sea-scented beach;
Three fields to cross till a farm appears;
A tap at the pane, the quick sharp scratch
And blue spurt of a lighted match,
And a voice less loud, thro' its joys and fears.
Than the two hearts beating each to each.

[H]

The splendour falls on castle walls
   And snowy summits old in story:
The long light shakes across the lakes,
   And the wild cataract leaps in glory.
Blow, bugle, blow, set the wild echoes flying,
Blow, bugle; answer, echoes, dying, dying, dying.

O hark, O hear! how thin and clear,
   And thinner, clearer, farther going!
O sweet and far from cliff and scar
   The horns of Elfland faintly blowing!
Blow, let us hear the purple glens replying:
Blow, bugle; answer, echoes, dying, dying, dying.

O love, they die in yon rich sky,
　　They faint on hill or field or river:
Our echoes roll from soul to soul,
　　And grow for ever and for ever.
Blow, bugle, blow, set the wild echoes flying,
And answer, echoes, answer, dying, dying, dying.

[I]

And, like a dying lady lean and pale,
Who totters forth, wrapp'd in a gauzy veil,
Out of her chamber, led by the insane
And feeble wanderings of her fading brain,
The moon arose up in the murky east
A white and shapeless mass.

[J]

He is made one with Nature: there is heard
His voice in all her music, from the moan
Of thunder to the song of night's sweet bird;
He is a presence to be felt and known
In darkness and in light, from herb and stone,
Spreading itself where'er that Power may move
Which has withdrawn his being to its own;
Which wields the world with never-wearied love,
Sustains it from beneath, and kindles it above.

　　.　　.　　.　　.　　.　　.　　.

The breath whose might I have invoked in song
Descends on me; my spirit's bark is driven
Far from the shore, far from the trembling throng
Whose sails were never to the tempest given;
The massy earth and spherèd skies are riven!
I am borne darkly, fearfully afar,
Whilst, burning through the inmost veil of heaven,
The soul of Adonais, like a star,
Beacons from the abode where the Eternal are.

6
Final judgement

Section E of the criticism in Chapter 7 consists of a summing up: a final judgement. All the critical analyses of the earlier sections lead to the conclusion expressed in the final paragraph. The meaning has been elucidated; the intention and tone have been explored; versification, prosody, diction and imagery have been examined. It is in the light of these detailed investigations that the critic reacts creatively to the poem as a whole.

The stages through which the critical process passes are these:

a What is the meaning of this poem?
b What is the poet's intention? What is the tone of the poem?
c How far does his style harmonise with his intention?
d What is the total impression that this poem makes on me?

It is in making our final judgements that the personal element in criticism comes most strongly to the fore. In all the earlier stages, rule and method can be applied, and our approach should be as objective as possible. But, as has been said before, there are two main aspects of the critic's work. He should first of all make clear to the reader the theme of a poem and the poet's attitude to it; and secondly, he should convey to the reader, firmly and vividly, the impressions that he has gained of the poem. It is in performing this second part of his work that the critic's personality comes into play with that of the poet. Provided that the earlier processes of the investigation have been honestly carried out, it is all to the good that the personal reactions of the critic should be strongly stated in his final judgement. Colourless, negative writing makes poor criticism; and vigour and honesty are looked for in the expression of what should be a well-informed, but nevertheless personal, opinion. After carrying out thorough investigations such as those described in the earlier chapters of this book, a critic has every right to state his personal opinions of a poem, for he is assured that he is expressing a judgement and not a prejudice, and is weighing each part against the whole. If, in making his final statement, he finds that a detail sticks so strongly in his mind as to colour his reactions to the whole, he will be right to mention it, since his survey has embraced every aspect of the poem, and should have secured for his final reading a correct perspective. What would have been a hasty impression at the beginning of the critical process, becomes a considered opinion at the end.

The great critics frequently present to their readers only their final judgements of a poem, omitting from their statements the earlier stages of their examination. It will usually be found, however, that it is possible to deduce from their writings, the criteria by which they are judging, and it is true to say that every great criticism of a particular poem, or of a poet's work as a whole, has emerged from a process similar to that described in this book. Here, for example, is Dr Johnson's criticism of Gray's *Elegy Written in a Country Churchyard*.

In the character of his Elegy I rejoice to concur with the common reader; for by the common sense of readers uncorrupted with literary prejudices, after all the refinements of subtlety and the dogmatism of learning, must be finally decided all claim to poetic honours. The 'Church-yard' abounds with images which find a mirror in every mind, and with sentiments to which every bosom returns an echo. The four stanzas beginning 'Yet even these bones', are to me original: I have never seen the notions in any other place; yet he that reads them here, persuades himself that he has always felt them. Had Gray written often thus, it had been in vain to blame, and useless to praise him.

It is clear from this criticism that Johnson looks for universality (*The 'Church-yard'* . . . *an echo*), and places a high value upon originality, which is not, however, to be confused with the merely startling or novel (last two sentences). It is clear, too, that although only general conclusions are given here, this final judgement rests on an earlier and close examination of detail, for in support of his claim that the Elegy is great, he immediately selects four stanzas of especial merit, thus practising his own sound doctrine: 'Critical remarks are not easily understood without examples.'

There can be no last word in criticism just as there can be no last word in history. Each age re-writes history, and each generation re-values the works of the past. Every great piece of criticism is a product of the personality of the critic as modified by the work of art with which he is dealing, and each great critic is to some extent a product of his own age. We turn back to the critics of the past for their help in understanding and appreciating poetry, but they cannot make up our minds for us. Look for a moment at these two judgements of John Donne and his followers (the so-called Metaphysical School), the first by Dr Johnson, and the second by T. S. Eliot.

1
Their thoughts are often new, but seldom natural; they are not obvious, but neither are they just; and the reader, far from wondering why he missed them, wonders more frequently by what perverseness of industry they were ever found. . . . The most heterogeneous ideas are yoked by violence together; nature and art ransacked for illustrations, comparisons and allusions; their learning instructs, and their subtlety surprises, but the reader commonly thinks his improvement dearly bought, and, though he sometimes admires, is seldom pleased. . . . Their wish was only to say what they hoped had never been said before.

2
It is to be observed that the language of these poets is as a rule simple and pure. . . . The structure of the sentences, on the other hand, is sometimes far from simple, but this is not a vice; it is a

fidelity to thought and feeling. The effect, at its best, is far less artificial than that of an ode by Gray. And as this fidelity induces variety of thought and feeling, so it induces variety of music. . . . Johnson has hit, perhaps by accident, on one of their peculiarities, when he observes that 'their attempts were always analytic'; he would not agree that, after the dissociation, they put the material together again in a new unity. . . . A thought to Donne was an experience; it modified his sensibility. When a poet's mind is perfectly equipped for its work, it is constantly amalgamating disparate experience; the ordinary man's experience is chaotic, irregular, fragmentary. The latter falls in love, or reads Spinoza, and these two experiences have nothing to do with each other, or with the noise of the typewriter or the smell of cooking; in the mind of the poet these experiences are always forming new wholes.

The disparity between those two judgements does not arise solely from the differing personalities of the two critics. It stems in part from the fact that Johnson's age believed with Pope that:

> True wit is Nature to advantage dressed,
> What oft was thought but ne'er so well expressed.

Whereas Eliot spoke for many of his contemporaries when he wrote:

We can only say that it appears likely that poets in our civilization as it exists at present, must be 'difficult'. Our civilization comprehends great variety and complexity, and this variety and complexity, playing upon a refined sensibility, must produce various and complex results. The poet must become more and more comprehensive, more allusive, more indirect, in order to force, to dislocate if necessary, language into his meaning.

Yet, different as the final judgements of the two critics are, Eliot constantly turns to Johnson in his interpretation of the Metaphysical poets, and cautions his readers against rejecting 'the criticism of Johnson (a dangerous person to disagree with) without having mastered it, without having assimilated the Johnsonian canons of taste'.

Such is the help that the great critics afford each other (and us); such is the value and justification of new judgements and constant re-valuations. In forming his own opinion and expressing the standards of *his* age, a critic of these poets in the twenty-first century will turn for help both to Dr Johnson and to Eliot.

It is not solely, however, the change in background and culture from age to age that differentiates the critics, and makes a 'final assessment' impossible. All critics, however objective their approach, are bound to express personal opinions, and many of the greatest have at times given rein to personal prejudices which, while not infrequently adding to the enjoyment of the reader, must be recognised for the prejudices they are, and discounted accordingly. Here, as an example, is Johnson's criticism of Milton's sonnets: 'They deserve not any particular criticism; for of the best it can only be said, that they are not bad.' Now Johnson was a very great critic indeed, yet on this point he misleads us entirely, and the reason is not far to seek, for we read immediately afterwards: 'The fabrick of a sonnet, however adapted to the Italian language, has never succeeded in ours, which, having greater variety of terminations, requires the rhymes to be often changed.' Nor should we expect a man who was afflicted by deafness to be sensitive to the delicate music of a sonnet.

Prejudice is often more than this, however, for it frequently arises not from an aesthetic weakness in the critic, but from a dislike of the poet's personality and beliefs. Johnson's bias against Milton as 'an acrimonious and surly republican' is frankly admitted by him, and we can easily allow for it in assessing the value of such adverse comments as arise from it. It should be noticed, too, that this prejudice did not prevent him from paying as noble praise to *Paradise Lost* as is to be found in the history of criticism. Similarly, Hazlitt's criticism of Byron's *Don Juan* is coloured by the critic's dislike of the poet's personality and views, and it is not difficult to detect this in the following extract.

The 'Don Juan' has indeed great power; but its power is owing to the force of the serious writing; and to the oddity of the contrast between that and the flashy passages with which it is interlarded. From the sublime to the ridiculous is but one step. You laugh and and are surprised that any one should turn round and 'travestie' himself: the drollery is in the utter discontinuity of ideas and feelings. He makes virtue serve as a foil to vice; 'dandyism' is (for want of any other) a variety of genius. A classical intoxication is followed by the splashing of the soda-water, by frothy effusions of ordinary bile. . . . The Noble Lord is almost the only writer who has prostituted his talent in this way. He hallows in order to desecrate; takes a pleasure in defacing the images of beauty his hands have wrought. . . . This is a most unaccountable anomaly. It is as if the eagle were to build its eyry in a common sewer, or the owl were seen soaring to the mid-day sun. Such a sight might make one laugh, but one would not wish or expect it to occur more than once.

Yet if these great men have their weaknesses, they are often great enough to triumph over them too. As a Radical, Hazlitt detested Scott's Toryism, and spoke of 'Sir Walter's gratuitous servility', but as a critic he spoke of Scott, the artist, in these terms: 'His worst is better than any other person's best. . . . His works (taken together) are almost like a new edition of human nature. This is indeed to be an author!' And later, in the same essay on Byron from which we have quoted, he referred to his own remarks as 'a strain of somewhat peevish invective'.

Enough has perhaps been said and quoted to justify these general points for the guidance of the critic in making his final judgement of a poet or a poem.

1 Having striven for objectivity in the earlier stages of his enquiry, the critic is entitled to express a personal judgement of the work with which he is dealing.

2 That personal judgement should be based on the detailed investigations already carried out, and these should be constantly referred to in arriving at the final statement.

3 Aesthetic considerations, not political or personal prejudices, should be paramount.
4 The final judgement should be vigorous, clear, and individual.
5 The standards by which the critic is judging should be made clear for the guidance of his readers. Mere praise or blame is insufficient; reasons should be given.

And finally, let us add for the encouragement of any reader who is disheartened by the amount of careful reading and hard work that is the inescapable preliminary of the critic's task, these words of Johnson: 'What we hope ever to do with ease, we may first learn to do with diligence.' No final judgement worth having can be made without careful thought, and nobody can become a true critic without constant practice and wide reading.

PRACTICAL WORK

1

Attempt to deduce from the following pieces of criticism, the critical standards upheld by their writers. In cases where a particular poem is criticised it should be studied carefully before the criticism is read.

a In this poem (*Lycidas*) there is no nature, for there is no truth; there is no art, for there is nothing new. Its form is that of a pastoral, easy, vulgar, and therefore disgusting: whatever images it can supply, are long ago exhausted, and its inherent improbability always forces dissatisfaction on the mind.

b Pastoral poetry not only amuses the fancy the most delightfully, but it is likewise more indebted to it than any other sort whatsoever. It transports us into a kind of fairy land, where our ears are soothed with the melody of birds, bleating flocks, and purling streams; our eyes enchanted with flowering meadows and springing greens; we are laid under cool shades, and entertained with all the sweets and freshness of nature. It is a dream, it is a vision, which we wish may be real, and we believe that it is true.

c Wordsworth's value is of another kind. Wordsworth has an insight into permanent sources of joy and consolation for mankind which Byron has not; his poetry gives us more which we may rest upon than Byron's, – more which we can rest upon now, and which men may rest upon always. I place Wordsworth's poetry, therefore, above Byron's on the whole, although in some points he was greatly Byron's inferior, and although Byron's poetry will always, probably, find more readers than Wordsworth's, and will give pleasure more easily.

d In a very different style of poetry is the 'Rime of the Ancient Mariner'; a ballad (says the advertisement) 'professedly written in imitation of the style, as well as the spirit of the elder poets.' We are tolerably conversant with the early English poets; and can discover no resemblance whatever, except in antiquated spelling and a few obsolete words. This piece appears to us perfectly original in style as well as in story. Many of the stanzas are laboriously beautiful; but in connection they are absurd or unintelligible. Our readers may exercise their ingenuity in attempting to unriddle what follows:

> The roaring wind, it roar'd far off
> It did not come anear, *etc, etc.*

We do not sufficiently understand the story to analyse it. It is a Dutch attempt at German sublimity. Genius has here been employed in producing a poem of little merit.

e Still, after more than a hundred years, 'The Ancient Mariner' is the wild thing of wonder, the captured star, which Coleridge brought in his hands to Alfoxden and showed to Dorothy and William Wordsworth. Not in the whole range of English poetry – not in Shakespeare himself – has the lyrical genius of our language spoken with such a

note. Its music is as effortless as its imagery. Its words do not
cumber it: exquisite words come to it, but it uses and
straightway forgets them. Not Shakespeare himself, unless
by snatches, so sublimated the lyrical tongue, or obtained
effects so magical by the barest necessary means. Take—

> The many men so beautiful!
> And they all dead did lie.

or

> The moving Moon went up the sky
> And nowhere did abide;
> Softly she was going up,
> And a star or two beside.

or

> The body of my brother's son
> Stood by me, knee to knee:
> The body and I pulled at one rope,
> But he said nought to me.

Here, and throughout, from the picture of the bride enter-
ing the hall to that of the home-coming in the moon-lit
harbour, every scene in the procession belongs to high
romance, yet each is conjured up with that economy of
touch we are wont to call classical. We forget almost,
listening to the voice, that there are such things as words.

> And now 'twas like all instruments,
> Now like a lonely flute;
> And now it is an angel's song
> That makes the heavens be mute.

If, in criticism, such an epithet be pardonable, we would
call that voice seraphic; if such a simile, we would liken it
to a seraph's musing, talking before the gate of Paradise in
the dawn.

2

What faults do you detect in the following passages of criticism?

[A]

> . . . He, above the rest
> In shape and gesture proudly eminent,
> Stood like a tower; his form had yet not lost
> All her original brightness, nor appeared
> Less than Archangel ruined, and the excess
> Of glory obscured: as when the sun new-risen
> Looks through the horizontal misty air
> Shorn of his beams, or from behind the moon,
> In dim eclipse, disastrous twilight sheds
> On half the nations, and with fear of change
> Perplexes monarchs. Darkened so, yet shone
> Above them all the Archangel; but his face
> Deep scars of thunder had entrenched, and care
> Sat on his faded cheek, but under brows
> Of dauntless courage, and considerate pride
> Waiting revenge.

Milton, a rebel himself, gives too sympathetic a description of the arch-rebel, and weakens the avowed purpose of his poem–'to justify the ways of God'–by so doing. This picture of Satan is a perversion of the truth, and as such to be condemned.

[B]

> Myself when young did eagerly frequent
> Doctor and Saint, and heard great Argument
>   About it and about: but evermore
> Came out by the same Door as in I went.
>
> With them the Seed of Wisdom did I sow,
> And with my own hand labour'd it to grow:
>   And this was all the Harvest that I reap'd–
> 'I came like Water, and like Wind I go.'
>
> Into this Universe, and *why* not knowing,
> Nor *whence*, like Water willy-nilly flowing:

And out of it, as Wind along the Waste,
I know not *whither*, willy-nilly blowing.

What, without asking, hither hurried *whence*?
And, without asking, *whither* hurried hence?
    Another, and another Cup to drown
The Memory of this Impertinence!

This is not poetry, but rhyming Fatalism. We have no patience with such an unmanly attitude to life; a namby-pamby taking refuge in intoxicating draughts, presumes to offer his advice on how to live.

[C]

We do lie beneath the grass
    In the moonlight, in the shade
Of the yew-tree. They that pass
    Hear us not. We are afraid
    They would envy our delight,
    In our graves by glow-worm night.
Come follow us, and smile as we;
    We sail to the rock in the ancient waves,
Where the snow falls by thousands into the sea,
    And the drowned and the shipwrecked have happy
        graves.

I feel that many of my readers will agree with me in considering this is a rather lovely little poem. A few may be put off by the apparent irregularity of some of the lines, but not, perhaps, many. Most will be too delighted by these happy fancies to be concerned with mere matters of scansion.

[D]

Had I a man's fair form, then might my sighs
    Be echoed swiftly through that ivory shell
    Thine ear, and find thy gentle heart; so well
Would passion arm me for the enterprize:
But ah! I am no knight whose foeman dies;
    No cuirass glistens on my bosom's swell;
    I am no happy shepherd of the dell

Whose lips have trembled with a maiden's eyes.
Yet must I dote upon thee,– call thee sweet,
  Sweeter by far than Hybla's honied roses
    When steep'd in dew rich to intoxication.
Ah! I will taste that dew, for me 'tis meet,
  And when the moon her pallid face discloses,
    I'll gather some by spells, and incantation.

This poem should never have been written. We cannot find a single beauty in it, nor discover one phrase that justifies its existence. We do not find it in any way moving and, having quoted it in full, shall spare our readers the *ennui* of perusing our reasons for this adverse judgement.

7
A piece of criticism

THE DARKLING THRUSH

I leant upon a coppice gate
   When Frost was spectre-gray,
And Winter's dregs made desolate
   The weakening eye of day.
The tangled bine-stems scored the sky
   Like strings of broken lyres,
And all mankind that haunted nigh
   Had sought their household fires.

The land's sharp features seemed to be
   The Century's corpse outleant,
His crypt the cloudy canopy,
   The wind his death-lament.
The ancient pulse of germ and birth
   Was shrunken hard and dry,
And every spirit upon earth
   Seemed fervourless as I.

At once a voice arose among
   The bleak twigs overhead
In full-hearted evensong
   Of joy illimited;
An aged thrush, frail, gaunt, and small,
   In blast-beruffled plume,
Had chosen thus to fling his soul
   Upon the growing gloom.

So little cause for carolings
   Of such ecstatic sound

> Was written on terrestrial things
>   Afar or nigh around,
>
> That I could think there trembled through
>   His happy good-night air
> Some blessed Hope, whereof he knew
>   And I was unaware.

THOMAS HARDY

CRITICISM

a★ This poem expresses forcibly the bleak desolation of a late afternoon in mid-winter, with the grim aspect of which the poet's own mood is in complete harmony.

b The first verse describes the isolation of the writer, a solitary human being gazing at the few dreary relics of summer that winter has preserved; and chilled, like the scene, by the grey frost.

In the second verse, the grimness of the poem is reinforced by the sudden enlargement of its scope. Hardy looks beyond the coppice and sees the whole landscape, so bare with the sharpness of death that he fancies that it is the dead body of the century. The earth lies beneath a cloudy vault, and the wind mourns the passing of an age. The vital principle of life is numbed, and the deadness of the world is matched by the apathy in the poet's mind.

The third stanza introduces a new element, for into the gloom of the evening bursts the song of a thrush; his joy contrasting poignantly with the desolate scene. So bare of comfort, however, is the earth, that, as the poet tells us in verse four, the only possible explanation of the thrush's outburst must be a secret known only to the bird, and shrouded darkly from the one human being who heard his song.

★The successive stages of the critical process are marked thus so that the reader can match this piece of work with the critical plan on page ix. It is not necessary to distinguish each stage in this manner in your own critical writing.

c Though an expression of a personal experience, and of the poet's own emotions, the theme and its treatment have a universal significance. The end of a year arouses in all men deep and often sad reflections. In this case, the remorseless impassiveness of the external world merges with man's melancholy, and the poem is the statement of a point of view that must be reckoned with: has the universe (or its creator) any interest in the life of the individual or, indeed, of the race; or is it merely a coolly ironical background before which man plays his part?

d The gravity of tone that such a theme demands is achieved throughout the poem. In every line we are conscious of the steady beat of the rising duple time, but the pattern is flexible. There is counterpointing in verse two, line seven, for example, where instead of the four full stresses that the previous pattern had led us to expect, we get,

> And every spirit upon earth.

In line three, verse three, there is a delightful modulation of the basic rhythm, the triple-time foot at the beginning of the line expressing the gathering impulse of the bird's song before the first full notes trill out.

> In a full-hearted evensong

In the same verse, counterpointing is again used to emphasise meaning. The exact description of the thrush conveyed by the three carefully-chosen adjectives is thrust home by the shift in stress pattern which brings three stressed syllables together and weights each of the adjectives.

> An aged thrush, frail, gaunt, and small.

The formal pattern of the stanzas is re-moulded whenever Hardy needs greater freedom of expression. The rhyme-scheme is rigid thus underlining the firmness of purpose and tone so apparent in the theme, but there is considerable use of run-on lines, especially in stanzas three and four, where the words run more freely in a quicker impulse of feeling.

The imagery and diction are remarkable for the way in which Hardy combines exactness of description with a demand on the imagination through the association of ideas. His use of adjectives and verbs is particularly striking. In almost every case the sense impression conveyed by the images sets up a chain of emotional and intellectual reactions (*eg* 'spectre-gray'; 'blast-beruffled'; 'the weakening eye of day'). This combination of sensuous with emotional and intellectual content is powerful in the vivid simile

> The tangled bine-stems scored the sky
> Like strings of broken lyres

while the imagery of verse two expresses the quintessence of the grim theme in the macabre suggestion of the second line: the corpse of the old, dead century seems to be leaning uneasily outwards, a ghastly reminder of the passage of time and the inevitability of death. The wind and the clouds complete the funereal note.

e Throughout, an imaginative realism is evident and the final impression left by this poem is a sombre one—as Hardy meant it to be. The song of the thrush carries only a limited comfort, for, to the poet, it remains as purposeless as life itself. While using the pathetic fallacy, Hardy grimly knows it for the fallacy it is. He stands in an ageing and barren world, gazing steadily and without self-pity at life as it is revealed to him at that moment; and communicating with dignity and sincerity what he feels and sees. The poem is a moving record of a man's tragic vision; a brave and memorable expression of 'the tears of things'.

8
Theories of poetry

Many theories about poetry, its nature and objectives, have been formulated, and although no single all-embracing and wholly satisfactory definition exists, much can be learnt by an examination of the theories put forward by the great poets and critics.

To enable the beginner to see his way clearly through the mass of critical material that is available, it is best to attempt an arrangement and classification, even at the cost of some sins of omission, and the risk of some arbitrary and dogmatic statements.

Theories about the nature and purpose of poetry tend to fall into one or the other of two wide classes: the hedonistic and the didactic. Those who belong to the former school of thought believe that the object of poetry is solely to give pleasure; those who belong to the latter consider that poetry should teach, though it must give pleasure, too, in the process of teaching. There are, of course, many shades of opinion within these schools. The extreme statement of the hedonistic point of view was made by Oscar Wilde when he said, 'There is no such thing as a moral or an immoral book; it is either well or badly written.' Somerset Maugham has said bluntly, 'Art is for delight.'

On the other side we have statements such as this by Sir Philip Sidney in his *Apologie for Poetrie*: 'It is that feigning of notable images of virtues, vices, or what else, with that delightful teaching, which must be the right describing note to know a Poet by.' Ben Jonson has a similar comment: 'Hence he is called a Poet, not he which writeth in measure (metre) only, but that feineth and formeth a fable, and writes things like the truth.' In the eighteenth century, Dr Johnson lent his authority to such a view: 'Nothing can please many, and please long, but just representations of general nature . . . the pleasures of sudden wonder are soon exhausted, and the mind can only repose on the stability of truth.' And lastly, here is Matthew Arnold's contribution to the controversy: 'Long ago, in speaking of Homer, I said that the noble and profound application of ideas to life is the most essential part of poetic greatness.'

This is a question which every reader must decide for himself, remembering that wide reading and hard thought will be necessary to the forming of a worth-while opinion. The following points form a basis for discussion of the problem and should be borne in mind:

1 Poetry written in accordance with the *extreme* hedonistic view is tiresome if prolonged.

2 Poetry written in accordance with the *extreme* didactic point of view is unreadable.

3 Comparatively little poetry, however, has been written in accordance with either of these critical extremes.

4 There is nothing in the *definition* of the hedonist school to prevent poetry from teaching, since if the object of poetry is solely to give pleasure, poetry which teaches may yet give pleasure to those who like to learn.

5 The terms 'instruct' or 'teach' may have a very wide sense. The learning of a multiplication table teaches us something, so does the reading of a Shakespearian tragedy.

6 The wisest upholders of the didactic approach have interpreted the above terms very widely, and have laid equal stress on teaching and delighting.

For example:

'Poetry is a speaking picture, with this end, to teach and delight' (SIR PHILIP SIDNEY).

'Poesy is a dulcet and gentle philosophy which leads on and

guides us by the hand to action with a ravishing delight and incredible sweetness' (BEN JONSON).

'Whatever professes to benefit by pleasing, must please at once' (DR JOHNSON).

'It is important, therefore, to hold fast to this: that poetry is at bottom a criticism of life; that the greatness of a poet lies in his powerful *and beautiful* application of ideas to life, to the question: How to live?' (MATTHEW ARNOLD).

7 Many thoughtful readers of poetry are agreed in rejecting the extremists on both sides, yet still they find with Coleridge that poetry which merely gives pleasure is fanciful, and poetry which combines the giving of pleasure with the discovery of truth is imaginative. They condemn poetry which too obviously and narrowly teaches, but, while enjoying that poetry which is full of 'natural magic', they find their deepest and most abiding satisfaction and pleasure in poetry which unites 'natural magic' and 'moral profundity' (Matthew Arnold). They expect, in other words, that a poem shall enlarge their experience and modify their sensibility before they will accord to it the title of great.

This is a very big critical problem, and in our rapid survey we have done no more than sketch in the lines along which an enquiry into it may proceed. It is a problem, however, to which constant attention must be given if the critic is to answer satisfactorily the questions, 'Why do I read poetry?' or 'What do I think of this poem?'

From the beginning of English critical theory (in the Elizabethan period) to the closing years of the nineteenth century, there were two main schools of criticism; the neo-Classical and the Romantic. The former was supreme until about 1798; the latter reigned from then until the turn of the nineteenth century. The neo-Classical critics—as their name implies—upheld the traditions of the classical writers of Greece and Rome, and believed that English poets would achieve greatness only by modelling their poetry on the example of

Greek and Roman poets. In his celebrated *Essay on Criticism*, Pope expressed the fundamental doctrines of the neo-Classical school.

[1]

> First follow NATURE and your judgement frame
> By her just standard, which is still the same:
> Unerring Nature, still divinely bright,
> One clear, unchanged, and universal light,
> Life, force and beauty, must to all impart,
> At once the source, and end, and test of art.

To many it will be surprising to find a neo-Classical poet and critic placing his first emphasis on Nature. Pope, however, did not mean by Nature what Wordsworth and the Romantics meant by it. To them it was external Nature – leaves, the green grass, hills, clouds, mountains and lakes – to him it was the general and universally observed truths of human nature and society. Very much, in other words, what Johnson meant by 'just representations of general nature'.

[2]

> Those RULES of old, discover'd, not devis'd,
> Are Nature still, but Nature methodiz'd;
> Nature, like liberty, is but restrain'd
> By the same laws which she herself ordain'd.
> Hear how learn'd Greece her useful rules indites,
> When to repress, and when indulge our flights.
> .   .   .   .
> You then whose judgement the right course would steer,
> Know well each ANCIENT'S proper character.

In those lines Pope advances two of the chief arguments of the neo-Classical faith. (*a*) That both in writing and in criticising poetry there are definite rules for the guidance of the poet and the critic. (*b*) These rules can be deduced from the literature of Greece and Rome, and should be observed by all writers. They are the plan whereby the poet shapes and executes his work; they are the yardstick by which the critic can measure the poet's success or failure.

[3]

> In wit, as Nature, what affects our hearts
> Is not th'exactness of peculiar parts;
> 'Tis not a lip, or eye, we beauty call,
> But the joint face and full result of all.
> Thus when we view some well-proportion'd dome
> (The world's just wonder, and ev'n thine, O Rome!)
> No single parts unequally surprise,
> All comes united to th'admiring eyes;
> No monstrous height, or breadth, or length appear;
> The whole at once is bold, and regular.
> .   .   .   .
> Most critics, fond of some subservient art,
> Still make the whole depend upon a part:
> They talk of principles but notions prize,
> And all to one lov'd folly sacrifice.
> Thus critics, of less judgement than caprice,
> Curious, not knowing, not exact but nice,
> Form short ideas; and offend in arts
> (As most in manners) by a love to parts.

Here, the poet pleads the cause of the characteristic classical virtues of moderation, symmetry, elegance, and proportion. In every poem and in every criticism, the means should be strictly subservient to the ends. A grand design should be apparent, and no detail, however beautiful in itself, which does not harmonise with that design is to be tolerated. We hear the same note again in Johnson's: 'Parts are not to be examined until the whole has been surveyed; there is a kind of intellectual remoteness necessary for the comprehension of any great work in its full design and its true proportions.'

The strength of neo-Classical poetry and criticism lay in these very real virtues of elegance, polish, and design. The best writers of the period were well-disciplined and thoughtful; they had a poised and urbane style, and a superb sense of tact and proportion. The weaker poets showed, however, a slavish adherence to rules with a consequent loss of inspiration; a refusal to experiment either in subject matter or diction, with a consequent hardening of style into a cliché-ridden and conventional jargon.

The Romantic school of poetry and criticism, though it had its eighteenth-century forebears, did not come into full fruit until after the publication of *Lyrical Ballads* in 1798. From then until the close of the Victorian Age Romanticism was supreme. It is not possible to find any single statement of the aims and ideals of this school which covers the whole ground. The celebrated Preface to the second edition of *Lyrical Ballads* (1800) concentrates on the diction and subject-matter of poetry, but from this and other writings of Wordsworth and Coleridge, as well as from the poetry and criticism of the other Romantics, we can extract statements and examples to put side by side with Pope's observations, and so contrast the two approaches to poetry and criticism.

1 Nature meant to the Romantics the external phenomena of the natural world and the influence of these on the spirit of man. They saw Nature as a direct emanation from God. Its beauty was divinely intended to move man's soul, and exalt him to new heights of virtue, by bringing him into communion with God.

> One impulse from a vernal wood
> May teach you more of man,
> Of moral evil and of good,
> Than all the sages can.
> WORDSWORTH *The Tables Turned*

> . . . For I have learned
> To look on nature, not as in the hour
> Of thoughtless youth; but hearing oftentimes
> The still, sad music of humanity,
> Nor harsh nor grating, though of ample power

> To chasten and subdue. And I have felt
> A presence that disturbs me with the joy
> Of elevated thoughts; a sense sublime
> Of something far more deeply interfused,
> Whose dwelling is the light of setting suns,
> And the round ocean and the living air,
> And the blue sky, and in the mind of man:
> A motion and a spirit, that impels
> All thinking things, all objects of all thought,
> And rolls through all things.
>
> WORDSWORTH   *Tintern Abbey*

Even where, as in Keats and Byron, the Romantics are not pantheistic in their approach to Nature, there is a passionate love of her beauty, and a sensitive apprehension of her awe and wonder, that is wholly lacking in the neo-Classicals.

2 They rejected *rules* whether drawn from ancient or from modern writers, and believed that great poetry resulted from the inspiration which seized those uniquely endowed beings called poets, and compelled them to express their feelings in a memorable and personal way. They were, that is to say, egoists, and subjective rather than objective in their approach to poetry.

For all good poetry is the spontaneous overflow of powerful feelings: but though this be true, Poems to which any value can be attached, were never produced on any variety of subjects but by a man, who being possessed of more than usual organic sensibility, had also thought long and deeply (WORDSWORTH).

If Poetry comes not as naturally as the leaves to a tree, it had better not come at all (KEATS).

3 The Romantics widened the scope of poetry by drawing their subject-matter from the most varied sources, and treating it subjectively: psychological studies of an individual man's mind; the legends of Greece and Rome; the history and myth of the Middle Ages; the simple tales of countrymen; all these and more, were grist for the

Romantics' mill. Wordsworth writes of the 'growth of a poet's mind' in *The Prelude*; Coleridge explores the furthest limits of fantasy in 'The Ancient Mariner'; Keats writes 'Lamia' and 'Isabella', going to Ancient Greece and Medieval Italy for his themes; Wordsworth recounts in noble poetry a simple and tragic country story in 'Michael'.

4 The Romantics strengthened poetry by a return to simplicity of diction. They threw off the clumsy periphrases and stilted idiom that had encumbered so much poetry at the end of the eighteenth century, and showed how glowing, how moving, and how imaginative the use of the simplest words could be in the right context. Let us hear Wordsworth's theory of this and see (at its best) his practice of his doctrine.

The principal object, then, which I proposed to myself in these Poems (*Lyrical Ballads*) was to choose incidents and situations from common life, and to relate or describe them, throughout, as far as was possible, in a selection of the language really used by men; and, at the same time to throw over them a certain colouring of the imagination, whereby ordinary things should be presented to the mind in an unusual way.

> If from the public way you turn your steps
> Up from the tumultuous brook of Green-head Ghyll,
> You will suppose that with an upright path
> Your feet must struggle; in such bold ascent
> The pastoral mountains front you, face to face.
> But, courage! for around that boisterous brook
> The mountains have all opened out themselves,
> And made a hidden valley of their own.
> No habitation can be seen: but they
> Who journey thither find themselves alone
> With a few sheep, with rocks and stones, and kites
> That overhead are sailing in the sky
>
> *Michael*

The same magnificent simplicity of diction catching, this time, an unearthly music, can be seen in Coleridge's

And now there came both mist and snow
And it grew wondrous cold:
And ice, mast-high, came floating by,
As green as emerald.

The Romantics at their greatest gave us music, wonder, exaltation, beauty, and expressed in their poetry a quickening of the human soul. Their faults were a tendency to 'purple patches' at the expense of the whole; a simplicity which degenerated into bathos; and a lowering of standards of craftsmanship in rhyme, metre, and construction.

This brief account of these two great schools of poetry and criticism has, of necessity, omitted many things, and dealt arbitrarily with others. The writer must leave it to your reading and the growth of your taste to piece out these imperfections. He has merely sought to give you an introduction to the subject. One last word must be said: avoid here, as everywhere else in criticism, a partisan's approach. It is not very helpful to try to decide whether the Romantics were 'better' than the neo-Classicals; they looked at poetry and at life differently and each had their strengths and their weaknesses.

Whether 'Modern Poetry' began in 1900, in 1913, when Ezra Pound published his 'injunctions' in *Poetry*, or in 1917 – when Eliot's *The Love Song of J. Alfred Prufrock* was first published – is arguable; but the fact that the twentieth century has produced so vast, so vigorous and so varied a body of poetry should make us cautious in generalising about its characteristics. Dominated in its earlier years by the twin – yet very different – giants, Yeats and Eliot, it also saw the work of Hardy, Lawrence, Owen, de la Mare, Auden, Day Lewis, Spender, MacNeice, Dylan Thomas and Betjeman. Nor, since the second world war, has there been any sign of dwindling vitality: R. S. Thomas, Ted Hughes, Elizabeth Jennings, Thom Gunn, Edwin Muir, Charles Causley, Philip Larkin . . . and these but a random selection of the names that are familiar to all readers of English poetry. Indeed, even to make such a selection is dangerous, opening the writer to the charge of bias or ignorance, since the omissions are palpable.

The whole point of risking such an arbitrary 'catalogue' is to demonstrate the fact that 'Modern Poetry' cannot be treated as if it consisted on one 'school', imposing a common identity on its members. English poetry has been a living, multi-faceted art throughout a period during which it has been too common for the poets to be lumped together as 'the Moderns' and treated as if they were practically identical in their aims and methods.

It would be outside the scope of this essentially practical book to include even a brief 'history' of English poetry since 1900. Nevertheless, since those who care for poetry will rightly want to attempt critical appreciation of what has been written in recent years, a few guide lines may be offered, even in note form. (More important than these notes, of course, are the examples of recent and contemporary poetry included for practical work.)

1   Even before the nineteenth century ended and, increasingly, in the years leading up to the first world war, many English poets became dissatisfied with their Victorian inheritance. The works of Tennyson and Browning seemed inappropriate 'models' for a generation that recognised the changed world in which they were living. Britain was no longer a predominantly agricultural and rural community and, indeed, had not been so for many years. Enormous economic, political and cultural changes had taken place. The volumes of 'Georgian Poetry' issued annually under the editorship of 'Eddie' Marsh, reflected an awareness of these changes; and reflected, too, a more 'intellectual' and experimental approach to poetry. It is unfortunate that the term 'Georgian Poetry' has come to be associated not with these pre-first-world-war pioneers of a new poetic but with the 'Georgians' of the 1920s who fought an ineffectual and misguided rearguard action against the changes that the work of Eliot and Pound had brought about in English

poetry. It is well to remember that the two greatest poets of the first world war – Edward Thomas and Wilfred Owen – were 'Georgians' in their search after truth and their experimental techniques; and important to recall that some of D. H. Lawrence's early verses were published in Marsh's annual volumes.

In the notes that he wrote for the intended Preface to his poems Wilfred Owen voiced ideas that have been echoed in the theory and practice of many very different twentieth century poets: 'Above all I am not concerned with Poetry.★ My subject is War, and the pity of War. The Poetry is in the pity.... All that a poet can do today is to warn. That is why the true Poets must be truthful.'

2 *Prufrock and Other Observations* (1917) quite clearly announced the 'new' poetry. Neglected or misunderstood, the volume made no great stir for a time; but when it was followed (in 1922) by *The Waste Land* Eliot's influence became paramount. As late as the 'thirties, academic critics were hostile to or contemptuous of Eliot's work; but the poets knew better. They recognised a major voice when they heard it; and Eliot's attitude to poetry (as expressed both in his poems and in his critical writings) has modified the art throughout this century. It seems possible to pick out three of his ideas which have been especially influential: he was insistent upon 'the integrity of poetry'; he believed that modern English poets must try to regain the 'unified sensibility' that he saw as having been the distinguishing mark of the Jacobeans and the Metaphysicals; and he saw the image ('the objective correlative') as central to poetry. This is not the place to explore the nature of his debt to the French Symbolists or to Ezra Pound. It is enough to stress that Eliot's poetry and criticism have changed the course of twentieth century poetry.

3 Many contemporary poets have affirmed that the most direct influence on their work has been that of W. B. Yeats

★Consider this surprising statement very carefully.

(1865–1939). Enormous as Eliot's achievement was, the work of the great Irishman which, in his middle and later years, sprang out of his response to his personal life and to the political life of Ireland spoke in a tradition immediately assimilable by the younger poets of his day and by poets who did not begin to write until well after his death. His range of subject matter and his immense honesty found a ready response in a generation that looked to the poets for comments on the events and issues of the times. They found in his work a welding of the 'private' and the 'public' man, inner struggles valiantly faced, a steady concern with the life of man – and all these expressed in sinewy verse, in diction and imagery that ranged from the starkly colloquial to the grandly rhetorical.

No critic who hopes to come to terms with modern poetry can neglect the influence of these two gigantic writers, Eliot and Yeats, who – together with Hopkins – changed the climate of opinion about what poetry is and about what it may be. The fences were removed by these great artists. After them, the field of poetry became once more the whole of human life.

4 Changes of this magnitude made many readers of poetry uncomfortable. They resented this interference with their cosy assumptions about poetry, longing for its return to its rural preoccupations, its word-painting and its established patterns. Poetry, like religion, they felt, should not be mixed up with everyday life. Hostility to the 'new poetry' has been widespread. Poets have been accused of wilful obscurity, of sordidness, of subversion. These charges have been bandied about more freely than in any previous age – a mark, perhaps, of how profound and rapid the changes have been.

5 After the second world war, once the bardic voice of Dylan Thomas was silenced, poetry went rather quiet. The poets of 'The Movement', for example, kept their heads down. Eccentricity was feared. The ruptured syntax that had

characterised the shock tactics of the *entre deux guerres* world was frowned upon. With no lessening of seriousness, with fine images and great skill, these post-war poets wrote a cooler poetry. There was some return to the traditional measures of English poetry, though resourceful experiment within these forms was frequent. The famous anthology, *New Lines* (1957) had much to say about 'rational structure and comprehensible language' as poetic ideals. Many recent critics have maintained that the 'modern movement' was a dead end. The Eliot-Pound influence and the 'public' poetry of the 'thirties written by 'committed' men – Auden, Spender, Day Lewis, and MacNeice, for example – was not in the central tradition of English poetry. The true line, these critics hold, runs through Hardy, Yeats, Graves and on into the poetry of the 'fifties and 'sixties, including the later work of those once-young poets who made the 'thirties ring with their passionate public poems. (In the reading list at the end of this book you will find listed some titles that will enable you to explore these ideas for yourself.)

6 It is best to end as we began, with a caution against hasty generalisations. Two of the most remarkable of contemporary poets, Ted Hughes and R. S. Thomas, cannot be fitted neatly into theories about 'schools' and 'lines'. Traditional influences are strong in their work, but they are unmistakably modern poets. Nor have we mentioned Basil Bunting, Sylvia Plath or Stevie Smith; or attempted to put Charles Causley's work into any critical niche. What is to be said of 'Pop Poetry' and the work of 'the Liverpool Poets'? The rich diversity of the present is as rewarding as ever, and the individual critic who seeks to explore it is embarking upon an exciting but pleasurable task.

To end this chapter on theory, here are statements by two great critics on the status and qualifications of the critic himself. Many when learning to judge poetry, have been discomfited by Ben Jonson's tart saying: 'To judge of poets is only the faculty of poets; and not of all poets, but the best.' There is, they have felt, an uncomfortable ring of truth in this remark. But it is, nevertheless, a half-truth, and a dangerous one at that. It isolates poetry from the life of 'the common reader' by proclaiming his inability to judge the works of his superiors; and poetry, if isolated from the life of men of ordinary powers who yet possess the imagination necessary to appreciate if not to create, soon becomes sterile and dies. The retort direct comes in this brief dialogue from Boswell's *Life of Johnson*:

BOSWELL. I mentioned Mallet's tragedy of 'Elvira', [and said that some friends] and myself had joined in writing a pamphlet . . . against it. That the mildness of Dempster's disposition had, however, relented; and he had candidly said, 'We have hardly a right to abuse this tragedy: for bad as it is, how vain should either of us be to write one not near so good.'

JOHNSON. Why, no, sir; this is not just reasoning. You *may* abuse a tragedy, though you cannot write one. You may scold a carpenter who has made you a bad table, though you cannot make a table. It is not your trade to make tables.

Adding merely that, even if we cannot make them, we should do our best to understand *how* tables are made, let us leave the last word to Dr Johnson.

9
Further material for practical criticism

1

Which of these poems are Romantic and which Classical?
Give full reasons for your answers, and state how far each of
them is typical of the strength or weakness of its particular
type.

[A]

> With many a pause and oft reverted eye
> I climb the coomb's ascent: sweet songsters near
> Warble in shade their wild-wood melody:
> Far off the unvarying cuckoo soothes my ear.
> Up scour the startling stragglers of the flock
> That on the green plots o'er precipices browse:
> From the forced fissures of the naked rock
> The yew-tree bursts! Beneath its dark green boughs
> (Mid which the may-thorn blends its blossoms white)
> Where broad smooth stones jut out in mossy seats,
> I rest:–and now have gained the topmost site.
> Ah! what a luxury of landscape meets
> My gaze! Proud towers, and cots more dear to me,
> Elm-shadow'd fields, and prospect-bounding sea!
> Deep sighs my lonely heart: I drop the tear:
> Enchanting spot! O were my Sara here!

[B]

> Of these the false Achitophel was first,
> A name to all succeeding ages curst:
> For close designs and crooked counsels fit.
> Sagacious, bold, and turbulent of wit,
> Restless, unfixt in principle and place,

In power unpleased, impatient of disgrace;
A fiery soul, which, working out its way,
Fretted the pigmy body to decay,
And o'er-informed the tenement of clay.
A daring pilot in extremity,
Pleased with the danger, when the waves went high
He sought the storms; but, for a calm unfit,
Would steer too near the sands to boast his wit.
Great wits are sure to madness near allied
And thin partitions do their bounds divide;
Else why should he, with wealth and honour blest,
Refuse his age the needful hours of rest?
Punish a body which he could not please,
Bankrupt of life, yet prodigal of ease?

[C]

Blow, blow, thou vernal gale!
Thy balm will not avail
To ease my aching breast;
Though thou the billows smooth,
Thy murmurs cannot soothe
My weary soul to rest.

Flow, flow, thou tuneful stream!
Infuse the easy dream
Into the peaceful soul;
But thou canst not compose
The tumult of my woes
Though soft thy waters roll.

Fade, fade ye flow'rets fair!
Gales, fan no more the air!
Ye streams, forget to glide!
Be hush'd each vernal strain;
Since nought can soothe my pain,
Nor mitigate her pride.

[D]

I stood tip-toe upon a little hill,
The air was cooling, and so very still,
That the sweet buds which with a modest pride

Pull droopingly, in slanting curve aside,
Their scantly leav'd, and finely tapering stems,
Had not yet lost those starry diadems
Caught from the early sobbing of the morn.
The clouds were pure and white as flocks new shorn,
And fresh from the clear brook; sweetly they slept
On the blue fields of heaven, and then there crept
A little noiseless noise among the leaves,
Born of the very sigh that silence heaves:
For not the faintest motion could be seen
Of all the shades that slanted o'er the green.

     .   .   .   .

I gazed awhile, and felt as light, and free
As though the fanning wings of Mercury
Had play'd upon my heels: I was light-hearted,
And many pleasures to my vision started;
So I straightway began to pluck a posey
Of luxuries bright, milky, soft and rosy.

[E]

After dark vapours have oppress'd our plains
  For a long dreary season, comes a day
  Born of the gentle South, and clears away
From the sick heavens all unseemly stains.
The anxious month, relieved of its pains,
  Takes as a long-lost right the feel of May;
  The eyelids with the passing coolness play
Like rose leaves with the drip of Summer rains.
The calmest thoughts come round us; as of leaves
  Budding—fruit ripening in stillness—Autumn suns
Smiling at eve upon the quiet sheaves—
Sweet Sappho's cheek—a smiling infant's breath—
  The gradual sand that through an hour-glass runs—
A woodland rivulet—a Poet's death.

[F]

  Know then thyself—presume not God to scan:
  The proper study of mankind is man.
  Placed on this isthmus of a middle state,

> A being darkly wise, and rudely great:
> With too much knowledge for the Sceptic side,
> With too much weakness for the Stoic's pride,
> He hangs between; in doubt to act, or rest;
> In doubt to deem himself a god, or beast;
> In doubt his mind or body to prefer;
> Born but to die, and reasoning but to err;
> Alike in ignorance, his reason such,
> Whether he thinks too little or too much:
> Chaos of thought and passion, all confused;
> Still by himself abused or disabused;
> Created half to rise, and half to fall;
> Great lord of all things, yet a prey to all;
> Sole judge of truth, in endless error hurled:
> The glory, jest, and riddle of the world!

2

Comment on the imagery and figures of speech employed in the following poems.

[A]

> I cannot see what flowers are at my feet,
>   Nor what soft incense hangs upon the boughs,
> But, in embalmed darkness guess each sweet
>   Wherewith the seasonable month endows
> The grass, the thicket, and the fruit-tree wild;
>   White hawthorn, and the pastoral eglantine;
>   Fast fading violets cover'd up in leaves;
> And mid-May's eldest child,
>   The coming musk-rose, full of dewy wine,
>   The murmurous haunt of flies on summer eves.

[B]

> Awake! for Morning in the Bowl of Night
> Has flung the Stone that puts the Stars to Flight:
> And Lo! the Hunter of the East has caught
> The Sultan's Turret in a Noose of Light.

[c]

Wake: the silver dusk returning
   Up the beach of darkness brims,
And the ship of sunrise burning
   Strands upon the eastern rims.

Wake: the vaulted shadow shatters,
   Trampled to the floor it spanned,
And the tent of night in tatters
   Straws the sky-pavilioned land.

[D]

Who ever comes to shroud me, do not harme
   Nor question much
That subtile wreath of haire, which crowns my arme;
The mystery, the signe you must not touch,
   For 'tis my outward Soule,
Viceroy to that, which then to heaven being gone,
   Will leave this to controule,
And keepe these limbes, her Provinces, from dissolution.

For if the sinewie thread my braine lets fall
   Through every part,
Can tye those parts, and make mee one of all;
These haires which upward grew, and strength and art
   Have from a better braine,
Can better do't; Except she meant that I
   By this should know my pain,
As prisoners then are manacled, when they are condemn'd
    to die.

What ere shee meant by it, bury it with me,
   For since I am
Loves martyre, it might breed idolatrie,
If into others hands these Reliques came;
   As 'twas humility
To afford to it all that a Soule can doe,
   So 'tis some bravery,
That since you would save none of mee, I bury some of you.

3

What is the poet's purpose in each of the following passages, and how far do you consider that he is helped or hindered by the versification that he employs?

[A]

> The world is too much with us; late and soon,
> Getting and spending, we lay waste our powers;
> Little we see in nature that is ours;
> We have given our hearts away, a sordid boon.
> This sea that bares her bosom to the moon,
> The winds that will be howling at all hours
> And are up-gathered now like sleeping flowers,
> For this, for everything, we are out of tune;
> It moves us not. – Great God, I'd rather be
> A Pagan suckled in a creed outworn;
> So might I, standing on this pleasant lea,
> Have glimpses that would make me less forlorn;
> Have sight of Proteus rising from the sea;
> Or hear old Triton blow his wreathèd horn.

[B]

> . . . Who am I?
> Why, one, sir, who is lodging with a friend
> Three streets off—he's a certain . . . how d'ye call?
> Master—a . . . Cosimo of the Medici,
> I' the house that caps the corner. Boh! you were best!
> Remember and tell me, the day you're hanged,
> How you affected such a gullet's gripe!
> But you, sir, it concerns you that your knaves
> Pick up a manner nor discredit you:
> Zooks, are we pilchards, that they sweep the streets
> And count fair prize what comes into their net?
> He's Judas to a tittle, that man is!
> Just a face! Why, sir, you make amends.
> Lord, I'm not angry! Bid your hangdogs go
> Drink out this quarter-florin to the health
> Of the mùnificent House that harbours me
> (And many more beside, lads! more beside!)
> And all's come square again.

[C]

The poplars are felled; farewell to the shade,
And the whispering sound of the cool colonnade!
The winds play no longer and sing in the leaves,
Nor Ouse on his bosom their image receives.

Twelve years have elapsed since I last took a view
Of my favourite field, and the bank where they grew;
And now in the grass behold they are laid,
And the tree is my seat that once lent me a shade!

The blackbird has fled to another retreat,
Where the hazels afford him a screen from the heat,
And the scene where his melody charmed me before
Resounds with his sweet-flowing ditty no more.

My fugitive years are all hasting away,
And I must ere long lie as lowly as they,
With a turf at my breast, and a stone at my head,
Ere another such grove shall arise in its stead.

'Tis a sight to engage me, if anything can,
To muse on the perishing pleasures of man;
Though his life be a dream, his enjoyments, I see,
Have a being less durable even than he.

[D]

Fear death?–to feel the fog in my throat,
    The mist in my face,
When the snows begin, and the blasts denote
    I am nearing the place,
The power of the night, the press of the storm,
    The post of the foe;
Where he stands, the Arch Fear in a visible form,
    Yet the strong man must go:
For the journey is done and the summit attained,
    And the barriers fall,
Though a battle's to fight ere the guerdon be gained,
    The reward of it all.
I was ever a fighter, so–one fight more,
    The best and the last!

I would hate that death bandaged my eyes, and forebore,
   And bade me creep past.
No! let me taste the whole of it, fare like my peers
   The heroes of old,
Bear the brunt, in a minute pay glad life's arrears
   Of pain, darkness and cold.
For sudden the worst turns the best to the brave,
   The black minute's at end,
And the elements' rage, the fiend-voices that rave,
   Shall dwindle, shall blend,
Shall change, shall become first a peace out of pain,
   Then a light, then thy breast,
O thou soul of my soul! I shall clasp thee again,
   And with God be the rest!

[E]

   . . . High in front advanced,
The brandished sword of God before them blazed,
Fierce as a comet; which with torrid heat,
And vapour as the Libyan air adust,
Began to parch that temperate clime; whereat
In either hand the hastening Angel caught
Our lingering parents, and to the eastern gate
Led them direct, and down the cliff as fast
To the subjected plain—then disappeared.
They, looking back, all the eastern side beheld
Of Paradise, so late their happy seat,
Waved over by that flaming brand, the gate
With dreadful faces thronged and fiery arms.
Some natural tears they dropped, but wiped them soon;
The world was all before them, where to choose
Their place of rest, and Providence their guide.
They, hand in hand, with wandering steps and slow,
Through Eden took their solitary way.

[F]

Jesus came from out the court-house door,
Stretched his hands above the passing poor.
Booth saw not, but led his queer ones there
Round and round the mighty court-house square.

Then, in an instant, all that blear review
Marched on spotless, clad in raiment new.
The lame were straightened, withered limbs uncurled
And blind eyes opened on a new, sweet world.

Oh, shout Salvation! It was good to see
Kings and Princes by the Lamb set free.
The banjos rattled and the tambourines
Jing-jing-jingled in the hands of Queens.

And when Booth halted by the curb for prayer
He saw his Master thro' the flag-filled air.
Christ came gently with a robe and crown
For Booth the soldier, while the throng knelt down.
He saw King Jesus. They were face to face,
And he knelt a-weeping in that holy place.
Are you washed in the blood of the Lamb?

4

Write appreciations of the following poems.

[A]

How sleep the brave, who sink to rest
By all their country's wishes blest!
When Spring, with dewy fingers cold,
Returns to deck their hallow'd mould,
She there shall dress a sweeter sod
Than Fancy's feet have ever trod.

By fairy hands their knell is rung;
By forms unseen their dirge is sung;
There Honour comes, a pilgrim grey,
To bless the turf that wraps their clay;
And Freedom shall awhile repair
To dwell, a weeping hermit, there!

[B]

It is not growing like a tree
  In bulk, doth make men better be;
Or standing long an oak, three hundred year,
To fall a log at last, dry, bald, and sere:

A lily of a day
Is fairer far, in May,
Although it fall and die that night;
It was the plant and flower of light.
In small proportions we just beauties see;
And in short measures, life may perfect be.

[C]

Lord, who createdst man in wealth and store,
Though foolishly he lost the same,
Decaying more and more,
Till he became
Most poor:
With thee
Oh let me rise
As Larks harmoniously,
And sing this day thy victories:
Then shall the fall further the flight in me.

[D]

Gather ye rose-buds while ye may,
Old Time is still a-flying,
And this same flower that smiles today,
Tomorrow will be dying.

The glorious lamp of heaven, the sun,
The higher he's a-getting.
The sooner will his race be run,
And nearer he's to setting.

That age is best which is the first,
When youth and blood are warmer;
But being spent, the worse, and worst
Times still succeed the former.

Then be not coy, but use your time;
And while ye may, go marry:
For having lost but once your prime,
You may for ever tarry.

[E]

Love bade me welcome: yet my soul drew back,
  Guilty of dust and sin.
But quick-eyed Love, observing me grow slack
  From my first entrance in,
Drew nearer to me, sweetly questioning
  If I lacked any thing.

A guest, I answered, worthy to be here:
  Love said: you shall be he.
I, the unkind, ungrateful? Ah my dear,
  I cannot look on thee.
Love took my hand, and smiling did reply,
  Who made the eyes but I?

Truth, Lord, but I have marred them: let my shame
  Go where it doth deserve.
And know you not, says Love, who bore the blame?
  My dear, then I will serve.
You must sit down, says Love, and taste my meat:
  So I did sit and eat.

[F]

Does the road wind uphill all the way?
  Yes, to the very end.
Will the day's journey take the whole long day?
  From morn to night, my friend.

But is there for the night a resting-place?
  A roof for when the slow, dark hours begin.
May not the darkness hide it from my face?
  You cannot miss that inn.

Shall I meet other wayfarers at night?
  Those who have gone before.
Then must I knock, or call when just in sight?
  They will not keep you waiting at that door.

Shall I find comfort, travel-sore and weak?
  Of labour you shall find the sum.
Will there be beds for me and all who seek?
  Yea, beds for all who come.

[G]

The first to climb the parapet
With 'cricket-ball' in either hand;
The first to vanish in the smoke
Of God-forsaken No-Man's land.
First at the wire and soonest through,
First at those red-mouthed hounds of hell
The Maxims, and the first to fall,—
They do their bit, and do it well.

Full sixty yards I've seen them throw
With all that nicety of aim
They learned on British cricket-fields.
Ah! bombing is a Briton's game!
Shell-hole to shell-hole, trench to trench,
'Lobbing them over,' with an eye
As true as though it *were* a game,
And friends were having tea close by.

Pull down some art-offending thing
Of carven stone, and in its stead
Let splendid bronze commemorate
These men, the living and the dead.
No figure of heroic size
Towering skyward like a god;
But just a lad who might have stepped
From any British bombing squad.

His shrapnel helmet set a-tilt,
His bombing waistcoat sagging low,
His rifle slung across his back:
Poised in the very act to throw.
And let some graven legend tell
Of those weird battles in the West
Wherein he put old skill to use
And played old games with sterner zest.

Thus should he stand, reminding those
In less believing days, perchance
How Britain's fighting cricketers
Helped bomb the Germans out of France.

And other eyes than ours would see;
And other hearts than ours would thrill,
And others say, as we have said:
'A sportsman and a soldier still.'

[H]

What passing-bells for these who die as cattle?
    Only the monstrous anger of the guns.
    Only the stuttering rifles' rapid rattle
Can patter out their hasty orisons.
No mockeries for them; no prayers nor bells,
    Nor any voice of mourning save the choirs,–
The shrill, demented choirs of wailing shells;
    And bugles calling for them from sad shires.

What candles may be held to speed them all?
    Not in the hands of boys, but in their eyes
Shall shine the holy glimmers of good-byes.
    The pallor of girls' brows shall be their pall;
Their flowers the tenderness of patient minds,
And each slow dusk a drawing-down of blinds.

[I]

It is not to be thought of that the Flood
Of British freedom, which to the open Sea
Of the world's praise from dark antiquity
Hath flowed, 'with pomp of waters, unwithstood,'
Road by which all might come and go that would,
And bear out freights of worth to foreign lands;
That this most famous Stream in Bogs and Sands
Should perish; and to evil and to good
Be lost for ever. In our Halls is hung
Armoury of the invincible Knights of old:
We must be free or die, who speak the tongue
That Shakespeare spake; the faith and morals hold
Which Milton held. In every thing we are sprung
Of Earth's first blood, have titles manifold.

[J]

The Sun does arise,
And make happy the skies;
The merry bells ring
To welcome the Spring;
The skylark and thrush,
The birds of the bush,
Sing louder around
To the bells' cheerful sound,
While our sports shall be seen
On the Echoing Green.

Old John, with white hair,
Does laugh away care,
Sitting under the oak,
Among the old folk.
They laugh at our play,
And soon they all say:
'Such, such were the joys
When we all, girls and boys,
In our youth-time were seen
On the Echoing Green.'

Till the little ones, weary,
No more can be merry;
The sun does descend,
And our sports have an end.
Round the laps of their mothers
Many sisters and brothers,
Like birds in their nest,
Are ready for rest,
And sport no more seen
On the darkening Green.

[K]

Proud word you never spoke, but you will speak
    Four not exempt from pride some future day.
Resting on one white hand a warm wet cheek
    Over my open volume you will say,
    'This man loved *me*!' then rise and trip away.

[L]

Cupid and my Campaspe play'd
At cards for kisses; Cupid paid:
He stakes his quiver, bow, and arrows,
His mother's doves, and team of sparrows;
Looses them too; then down he throws
The coral of his lip, the rose
Growing on's cheek (but none knows how);
With these, the crystal of his brow,
And then the dimple of his chin;
All these did my Campaspe win:
At last he set her both his eyes—
She won, and Cupid blind did rise.
O Love! has she done this to thee?
What shall, alas! become of me?

5

Make critical comparisons between the following linked
poems, paying close attention to similarities and differences
in theme, tone and treatment.

[A]

THE HAWK IN THE RAIN

I drown in the drumming ploughland, I drag up
Heel after heel from the swallowing of the earth's mouth,
From the clay that clutches my each step to the ankle
With the habit of the dogged grave, but the hawk —

Effortlessly at height hangs his still eye.
His wings hold all creation in a weightless quiet,
Steady as a hallucination in the streaming air.
While banging wind kills these stubborn hedges,

Thumbs my eyes, throws my breath, tackles my heart,
And rain hacks my head to the bone, the hawk hangs
The diamond point of will that polestars
The sea drowner's endurance: and I,

Bloodily grabbed dazed last-moment-counting
Morsel in the earth's mouth, strain towards the master-

> Fulcrum of violence where the hawk hangs still.
> That maybe in his own time meets the weather
>
> Coming the wrong way, suffers the air, hurled upside down,
> Fall from his eye, the ponderous shires crash on him,
> The horizon trap him; the round angelic eye
> Smashed, mix his heart's blood with the mire of the land.

TED HUGHES★

[B]

THE WINDHOVER: TO CHRIST OUR LORD

> I caught this morning morning's minion, kingdom of
>   daylight's dauphin, dapple-dawn-drawn Falcon, in his
>   riding
> Of the rolling level underneath him steady air, and striding
> High there, how he rung upon the rein of a wimpling wing
> In his ecstasy! then off, off forth on swing,
>   As a skate's heel sweeps smooth on a bow-bend: the hurl
>   and gliding
> Rebuffed the big wind. My heart in hiding
> Stirred for a bird,–the achieve of, the mastery of the thing!
>
> Brute beauty and valour and act, oh, air, pride, plume, here
>   Buckle! AND the fire that breaks from thee then, a billion
> Times told lovelier, more dangerous, O my chevalier!
>
>   No wonder of it: shéer plód makes plough down sillion
> Shine, and blue-bleak embers, ah my dear,
>   Fall, gall themselves, and gash gold-vermilion.

GERARD MANLEY HOPKINS★

[C]

A REFUSAL TO MOURN THE DEATH, BY FIRE,
OF A CHILD IN LONDON

> Never until the mankind making
> Bird beast and flower
> Fathering and all humbling darkness
> Tells with silence the last light breaking

★'Hawk Roosting', another poem by Ted Hughes, provides further vivid material
for comparison with those two.

And the still hour
Is come of the sea tumbling in harness

And I must enter again the round
Zion of the water bead
And the synagogue of the ear of corn
Shall I let pray the shadow of a sound
Or sow my salt seed
In the least valley of sackcloth to mourn

The majesty and burning of the child's death.
I shall not murder
The mankind of her going with a grave truth
Nor blaspheme down the stations of the breath
With any further
Elegy of innocence and youth.

Deep with the first dead lies London's daughter,
Robed in the long friends,
The grains beyond age, the dark veins of her mother,
Secret by the unmourning water
Of the riding Thames.
After the first death, there is no other.

DYLAN THOMAS

[D]

A CHILD ILL

Oh, little body, do not die.
    The soul looks out through wide blue eyes
So questioningly into mine,
    That my tormented soul replies:

'Oh, little body, do not die.
    You hold the soul that talks to me
Although our conversation be
    As wordless as the windy sky,'

So looked my father at the last
    Right in my soul, before he died,
Though words we spoke went heedless past
    As London traffic-roar outside.

And now the same blue eyes I see
　　Look through me from a little son,
So questioningly, so searchingly
　　That youthfulness and age are one.

My father looked at me and died
　　Before my soul made full reply.
Lord, leave this other Light alight—
　　Oh, little body, do not die.

SIR JOHN BETJEMAN

[E]

HI!

Hi! handsome hunting man
Fire your little gun.
Bang! Now the animal
Is dead and dumb and done.
Nevermore to peep again, creep again, leap again,
Eat or sleep or drink again, Oh, what fun!

WALTER DE LA MARE

[F]

I SAW A JOLLY HUNTER

I saw a jolly hunter
　　With a jolly gun
Walking in the country
　　In the jolly sun.

In the jolly meadow
　　Sat a jolly hare
Saw the jolly hunter
　　Took jolly care.

Hunter jolly eager—
　　Sight of jolly prey.
Forgot gun pointing
　　Wrong jolly way.

Jolly hunter jolly head
　　Over heels gone.
Jolly old safety-catch
　　Not jolly on.

Bang went the jolly gun.
    Hunter jolly dead.
Jolly hare got clean away.
    Jolly good, I said.
CHARLES CAUSLEY

[G]

PISCES

Who said to the trout,
You shall die on Good Friday
To be food for a man
And his pretty lady?

It was I, said God,
Who formed the roses
In the delicate flesh
And the tooth that bruises.
R. S. THOMAS

6

Write appreciations of the following poems.

[A]

GRAVE BY A HOLM-OAK

You lie there, Anna,
In your grave now,
Under a snow-sky,
You lie there now.

Where have the dead gone?
Where do they live now?
Not in the grave, they say,
Then where now?

Tell me, tell me,
Is it where I may go?
Ask not, cries the holm-oak,
Weep, says snow.
STEVIE SMITH

SNOW

I wake up early
And go to sleep late
And think in between of my terrible fate.

I dream when I sleep,
Which is little, I know,
Of the childish games that I played in the snow.

O, childhood, so far,
And life not so long:
The race to the swift and the fight to the strong.

The wise men and good men
All lie in their hearts,
And try to cast humans in angelic parts.

Good angels; bad angels;
You've got to be one:
Before you know which, your life has gone.

The snow of the past
Was a playground then:
It's just one more plague in the world of men.

The poets all tell us
Our childhood snow
Shines bright in our journey as onward we go.

Chaste white in the dawn
Of life, melting so fast:
Snow, like our years and youth, cannot last.

So, white angel, black angel,
Act out your role—
One of you dominates each human soul.

The flames of the lost ones,
The crowns of the saved,
The golden mosaics with which heaven is paved:

I'd change all the symbols
That religious men teach
For the snow of my childhood – whatever they preach.

They preach their stern lessons
Of right and of wrong:
The snows of the spring are the notes of *my* song.

SAM HOLROYD

[c]

SONG

This that I give and take,
This that I keep and break,
Is and is not my own
But lives in itself alone,
Yet is between us two,
Mine only in the breaking,
It all in the remaking,
Doing what I undo.

With it all must be well,
There where the invisible
Loom sweetly plies its trade.
All made there is well-made
So be it between us two;
A giving be our taking,
A making our unmaking,
A doing what we undo.

EDWIN MUIR

[D]

WHAT THE CHAIRMAN TOLD TOM

Poetry? It's a hobby.
I run model trains.
Mr Shaw there breeds pigeons.

It's not work. You don't sweat.
Nobody pays for it.
You *could* advertise soap.

169

Art, that's opera; or repertory –
The Desert Song.
Nancy was in the chorus.

But to ask for twelve pounds a week –
married, aren't you? –
you've got a nerve.

How could I look a bus conductor
in the face
if I paid you twelve pounds?

Who says it's poetry, anyhow?
My ten year old
can do it *and* rhyme.

I get three thousand and expenses,
a car, vouchers,
but I'm an accountant.

They do what I tell them,
my company.
What do *you* do?

Nasty little words, nasty long words,
It's unhealthy.
I want to wash when I meet a poet.

They're Reds, addicts,
all delinquents.
What you write is rot.

Mr Hines says so, and he's a schoolteacher,
He ought to know.
Go and find *work*.

BASIL BUNTING

[E]

SHORT ODE TO THE CUCKOO

No one now imagines you answer idle questions
– *How long shall I live? How long remain single?*
Will butter be cheaper? – nor does your shout make
husbands uneasy.

Compared with arias by the great performers
such as the merle, your two-note act is kid-stuff:
our most hardened crooks are sincerely shocked by
    your nesting habits.

Science, Aesthetics, Ethics, may huff and puff but they
cannot extinguish your magic: you marvel
the commuter as you wondered the savage.
    Hence, in my diary,

where I normally enter nothing but social
engagements and, lately, the death of friends, I
scribble year after year when I first hear you,
    of a holy moment.

W. H. AUDEN

Appendix

TECHNICAL TERMS

1 PROSODY

Here are the four commonest feet in English poetry:

1 Iambus $\times$ / (tee-*tum*)
2 Trochee / $\times$ (*tum*-tee)
3 Anapáest $\times \times$ / (tee-tee-*tum*)
4 Dactyl / $\times \times$ (*tum*-tee-tee)

Occasionally the following are used:

5 Amphibrach $\times$ / $\times$
6 Spondee / /
7 Pyrrhic $\times \times$

In Sprung Rhythm and Free Verse, stress is still the basis of the rhythm; but here, three, four, or more slack syllables may be grouped with each stressed one. (See Chapter 3.)

The metre of a poem depends on the number of feet to the line and the pattern of the stanzas as well as the kind of feet used.

A line containing one   foot is called a monometer.

,, ,,	,,	two	feet ,,	,,	,, dimeter.
,, ,,	,,	three	,, ,,	,,	,, trimeter.
,, ,,	,,	four	,, ,,	,,	,, tetrameter.
,, ,,	,,	five	,, ,,	,,	,, pentameter.
,, ,,	,,	six	,, ,,	,,	an hexameter.
,, ,,	,,	seven	,, ,,	,,	,, heptameter.
,, ,,	,,	eight	,, ,,	,,	,, octameter.

The chief English Stanzas are:

a Ballad Metre

Four line stanzas consisting of alternate iambic tetrameters
and trimeters and rhyming a b c b.

> Childe Maurice hunted the Silver Wood,
>   He whistled and he sang:
> 'I think I see the woman yonder
>   That I have lovéd lang.'
>   *Childe Maurice*

b The Heroic Couplet

Iambic pentameters rhyming aa bb, *etc* (*ie* in couplets).

> And now, unveiled, the toilet stands displayed,
> Each silver vase in mystic order laid,
> First, robed in white, the Nymph intent adores,
> With head uncovered, the Cosmetic Pow'rs.
>   *The Rape of the Lock*

c Blank Verse

Unrhymed iambic pentameters.

> Of man's first disobedience and the fruit
> Of that forbidden Tree, whose mortal taste
> Brought death into the world and all our woe,
> With loss of Eden, till one greater Man
> Restore us, and regain the blissful seat,
> Sing, Heavenly Muse.
>   *Paradise Lost*

d Spenserian Stanza

Nine-lined stanza consisting of eight iambic pentameters
followed by one Alexandrine (iambic hexameter). Rhymes
ab ab bc bc c.

> Lo I the man, whose Muse whilome did maske,
> As time her taught, in lowly Shepheards weeds!
> Am now enforst a far unfitter taske,
> For trumpets stern to change mine Oaten reeds,
> And sing of Knights and Ladies gentle deeds!

> Whose prayses having slept in silence long,
> Me, all too meane, the sacred Muse areeds
> To blazon broad amongst her learned throng:
> Fierce warres and faithfull loves shall moralize my song.
>
> *Faerie Queene*

e Sonnet

Petrarchan, Shakespearian, or Miltonic. (See Chapter 3.)

f Rhyme Royal

Seven iambic pentameters rhyming ab ab bc c.

> The double sorwe of Troilus to tellen,
> That was the kyng Priamus sone of Troye,
> In lovynge, how his aventures fellen
> From wo to wele, and after out of joie,
> My purpose is, er that I parte fro ye.
> Thesiphone, thow help me for t'endite
> Thise woful vers, that wepen as I write.
>
> *Troilus and Criseyde*

g Ottava Rima

Eight iambic pentameters rhyming ab ab ab cc.

> My poem's epic, and is meant to be
>   Divided in twelve books! each book containing,
> With love, and war, a heavy gale at sea,
>   A list of ships, and captains, and kings reigning,
> New characters; the episodes are three:
>   A panoramic view of hell's in training,
> After the style of Virgil and of Homer,
> So that my name of Epic's no misnomer.
>
> *Don Juan*

Technical devices:

a Caesura

The pause dividing a line of verse into two parts.

> Satan exalted sat ‖ by merit raised.
>
> *Paradise Lost*

b End-stopped line
A line ending in a pause.

> Whereto with speedy words the Arch-Fiend replied:
> Fallen Cherub, to be weak is miserable,
> Doing or suffering.
>
> *Paradise Lost*

c Run-on line (enjambment)
Here the sense comes straight through without a pause from
the end of one line to the beginning of the next.

> But see! the angry victor hath recalled
>
> His ministers of vengeance and pursuit
>
> Back to the gates of Heaven.
>
> *Paradise Lost*

d Weak Ending
The slack, or unstressed, tenth syllable in an unrhymed
iambic pentameter.

> Since what I am to say must be but that
> Which contradicts my accusation, and
> But what comes from myself.
>
> *The Winter's Tale*

e Feminine Ending
The slack, or unstressed, eleventh syllable in an unrhymed
iambic pentameter.

> If you would not so,
> You pity not the state, nor the remembrance
> Of his most sovereign name.
>
> *The Winter's Tale*

2 KINDS OF POETRY

a *Lyrical Poetry*

Short and intensely personal and passionate poems (*eg* sonnet, ode (extended lyric), elegy, song).

b *Dramatic Poetry*

Comedy, Tragedy, Masque, Monodrama. All these have in common the use of characters and an attempt to represent the speech and actions of human beings.

c *Narrative Poetry*

Poetry which tells a story (*eg* short tales in verse; epic; romance).

d *Didactic Poetry*

Poetry which teaches. Allegory and Satire.

e *Descriptive Poetry*

Direct description of scenes and places as well as:

Pastoral: poetry dealing with a 'golden age' in which the main characters are idealised shepherds and shepherdesses.

Eclogue: consisting of dialogues between 'pastoral' shepherds.

Idyll: smooth and idealised description of rural or domestic life.

f *Humorous Poetry*

Burlesque: poetry which ridicules ideas or things; mock-heroic.

Parody: poetry which *imitates* the style of another poet with the intent to poke fun at it.

Note

The student requiring more detailed information about technical terms is recommended to consult R. F. Brewer's *Art of Versification and the Technicalities of Poetry*, and H. W. Fowler's *Dictionary of Modern English Usage*, both of which the writer has used in making this Appendix.

A short reading list

COLERIDGE: *Biographia Literaria (especially Chapter XIV).*
P. GURREY: *Appreciation of Poetry.*
GRAHAM HOUGH: *Image and Experience.*
JOHNSON: *The Lives of the Poets (especially Lives of Milton, Pope and Gray).*
KEATS: *Letters of John Keats.*
W. P. KER: *The Art of Poetry.*
FRANK KERMODE: *Romantic Image.*
C. DAY LEWIS: *Poetry for You.*
D. S. MACCOLL: *Rhythm in English Verse, Prose and Speech. (English Association Essays and Studies, Vol. V.)*
J. MIDDLETON MURRY: *The Problem of Style.*
GEORGE SAINTSBURY: *A History of English Criticism* and *A History of English Prosody.*
J. H. SCOTT: *Rhythmic Verse.*
SHELLEY: *A Defence of Poetry.*
E. A. SONNENSCHEIN: *What is Rhythm?*
E. M. W. TILLYARD: *Poetry Direct and Oblique.*
WORDSWORTH: *Preface to 'Lyrical Ballads'.*

See, too, books referred to in the text.

Sources of the unattributed extracts set for practical work

CHAPTER 1

EXERCISE 1

a From 'The Bard'– GRAY.

b From 'Kubla Khan'– COLERIDGE.

c 'Call for the robin-redbreast'– WEBSTER.

d From 'For Annie'– POE.

e From 'A Garden'– MARVELL.

f From 'Elegy to the Memory of an Unfortunate Lady'– POPE

g Sonnet CVI– SHAKESPEARE.

EXERCISE 2

a 'So we'll go no more a-roving'– BYRON.

b 'The Last Word'– ARNOLD.

c 'Written in March'– WORDSWORTH.

d 'Jenny Kiss'd Me'– LEIGH HUNT.

e 'Song'– HENRY REYNOLDS.

f 'Timber'– VAUGHAN.

g 'When the Assault was intended to the City'– MILTON.

CHAPTER 2

EXERCISE 1

a 'On the Loss of "The Royal George" '– COWPER.

b 'The Patriot'– BROWNING.

c 'As Frail as Dishes'– HOOD.

d 'To Dianeme'– HERRICK.

e 'On his Blindness'– MILTON.

EXERCISE 2

a 'To his Flocks'– CONSTABLE.

b 'The Humble Tutor'– HALL.

c 'Ozymandias'– SHELLEY.

d 'Even such is Time'– RALEIGH.

e 'The Windmill'– LONGFELLOW.

EXERCISE 3

a 'Proud Maisie'– SCOTT.

b 'The Express'– SPENDER.

c 'The Passionate Shepherd'– MARLOWE.

d 'Song'– DIXON.

e 'If, in the month of dark December'– BYRON.

CHAPTER 3

EXERCISE 1

a From 'The Epistle to Arbuthnot'– POPE.

b From 'The Deserted Village'– GOLDSMITH.

c From 'London'– JOHNSON.

d From 'Troilus and Cressida'– SHAKESPEARE.

e From 'The Task'– COWPER.

f From 'Hamlet'– SHAKESPEARE.

g 'On first looking into Chapman's Homer'– KEATS.

h 'Leave Me, O Love'– SIDNEY.

EXERCISE 2

a From 'The Traveller'– GOLDSMITH.

b From 'Locksley Hall'– TENNYSON.

c From 'The Destruction of Sennacherib'– BYRON.

d From 'The Lost Leader'– BROWNING.

e From 'The Windhover'– HOPKINS.

EXERCISE 3

a From 'The Triple Foole'– DONNE.

b From 'Song'– DONNE.

c 'The Pillar of Fame'– HERRICK.

d From 'Oh, talk not to me of a name great in story'– BYRON.

EXERCISE 5

a From 'Paradise Lost'–MILTON.

b From 'The Inferno'–DANTE.

c From 'Hyperion'–KEATS.

d From 'Lamia'–KEATS.

e From 'Paradise Lost'–MILTON.

CHAPTER 5

a From 'The Rubaiyat of Omar Khayyam'–FITZGERALD.

b 'Break, break, break'–TENNYSON.

c 'The Subjugation of Switzerland'–WORDSWORTH.

d From 'High Tide on the Coast of Lincolnshire'–JEAN INGELOW.

e 'Requiescat'–ARNOLD.

f From 'Samson Agonistes'–MILTON.

g 'Meeting at Night'–BROWNING.

h From 'The Princess'–TENNYSON.

i From 'The Moon'–SHELLEY.

j From 'Adonais'–SHELLEY.

CHAPTER 6

EXERCISE 1

Critical extracts by:

a DR JOHNSON.

b STEELE.

c ARNOLD.

d SOUTHEY.

e 'Q'.

EXERCISE 2

a From 'Paradise Lost'–MILTON.

b From 'The Rubaiyat of Omar Khayyam'–FITZGERALD.

c 'Sibylla's Dirge'–BEDDOES.

d Sonnet 'To ★★★'–KEATS.

CHAPTER 9

EXERCISE 1

a 'Lines'–COLERIDGE.

b From 'Absalom and Achitophel'–DRYDEN.

c 'Blow, blow, thou vernal gale!'–BEATTIE.

d From 'I stood tip-toe'–KEATS.

e Sonnet: 'After dark vapours'–KEATS.

f From 'Essay On Man'–POPE.

EXERCISE 2

a From 'Ode to a Nightingale'–KEATS.

b From 'The Rubaiyat of Omar Khayyam'–FITZGERALD.

c From 'A Shropshire Lad'–A. E. HOUSMAN.

d 'The Funerall'–DONNE.

EXERCISE 3

a Sonnet: 'The world is too much with us'–WORDSWORTH.

b From 'Fra Lippo Lippi'–BROWNING.

c 'The Poplar Field'–COWPER.

d 'Prospice'–BROWNING.

e From 'Paradise Lost'–MILTON.

f From 'General William Booth enters into Heaven'–VACHEL LINDSAY.

EXERCISE 4

a 'How sleep the brave'–COLLINS.

b 'It is not growing like a tree'–BEN JONSON.

c 'Easter Wings'–HERBERT.

d 'Gather ye rose-buds'–HERRICK.

e 'Love'–HERBERT.

f 'Uphill'–CHRISTINA ROSSETTI.

g 'The first to climb the parapet'–ANON.

h 'Anthem for Doomed Youth'–OWEN.

i Sonnet–WORDSWORTH.

j 'The Echoing Green'–BLAKE.

k 'Proud word you never spoke'–LANDOR.

l 'Cupid and Campaspe'–LYLY.